Eliminating the IMF

Imad A. Moosa • Nisreen Moosa

Eliminating the IMF

An Analysis of the Debate to Keep,
Reform or Abolish the Fund

Imad A. Moosa
School of Economics
RMIT School of Economics
Melbourne, VIC, Australia

Nisreen Moosa
University of South Australia
Adelaide, SA, Australia

ISBN 978-3-030-05760-2   ISBN 978-3-030-05761-9   (eBook)
https://doi.org/10.1007/978-3-030-05761-9

Library of Congress Control Number: 2018968425

This Palgrave Macmillan imprint is published by the registered company Springer Nature Switzerland AG
The registered company address is: Gewerbestrasse 11, 6330 Cham, Switzerland

To Danny, Ryan and Ivy

PREFACE

This book is written in the normative, rather than positive, tradition to point out what ought to be, rather than what is, with respect to the question of what to do about the International Monetary Fund (IMF). Although the views on this issue vary, they fall under three alternative courses of action: keep, reform or abolish. Calls for the preservation of the IMF are made by those who want to maintain the status quo, those who want to introduce cosmetic changes and those who want the IMF to expand and its mandate broadened. Those calling for reforming the IMF put forward various suggestions that boil down to limiting the damage inflicted by IMF conditionality on poor countries. Then there are those who believe that the IMF should be abolished, either because the purpose for which it was created is no longer there or because the Fund has done so much damage and inflicted so much pain on the developing world that no amount of reform would suffice.

The book is divided into seven chapters. The main issue under consideration, which is what to do about the IMF, is dealt with in Chap. 6, before the concluding thoughts are outlined in Chap. 7. To put the debate into perspective, some background discussion of the issues motivating each course of action (keep, reform or abolish) is necessary. In Chap. 1 we present a self-portrait of the IMF, outlining its history and functions from the perspective of the Fund itself. In Chaps. 2 and 3 we evaluate the principles guiding IMF operations, including the ten commandments of the Washington Consensus and some other variants that can be summarised in three words: liberalisation, privatisation and deregulation. In Chap. 4 we describe some violent reactions to IMF operations (taking the form of riots, civil unrest and mass demonstrations) and explain why the conditionality associated with IMF loans triggers violent popular reactions in the borrowing countries. Chapter 5 deals with the effects of IMF operations on social expenditure. The conclusion that we reach is that most of the world would be better off without the IMF.

This book is written by a father and daughter. The father is an economist with first-hand information on some of the issues discussed in this book, obtained through employment and advisory roles. The daughter is a clinical health scientist-turned health economist. She primarily wrote the parts of the book dealing with the effects of IMF operations on health and education. The book is an extension of the propositions put forward in two articles that were published in a special issue on the IMF of *Management and Economics Research Journal*: "The Consequences of IMF Conditionality for Government Expenditure on Health" and "Has the IMF Outlived its Usefulness or Gone Past its 'Use-by' Date?"

Writing this book would not have been possible without the help and encouragement we received from family, friends and colleagues. Our utmost gratitude must go to our families who had to bear the opportunity cost of writing the book. Therefore our thanks go to Afaf, Mike, Danny, Ryan and Ivy. Afaf used her expertise to draw the diagrams shown in the book, something that we could not have done without her help. We received help and support from Vikash Ramiah, Brien McDonald, Monica Tan, Marie-Anne Cam, Bob Parsons, Greg O'Brien, Greg Bailey, Paul Rule, Peter Murphy, Bob Brownlee and Ron Ripple. We are grateful to Bill Breen for serious comments on some parts of the manuscript. We also thank Kevin Dowd for his insightful comments on the proposal and his never-ending intellectual support. All remaining errors and omissions are entirely ours.

Melbourne, VIC, Australia   Imad A. Moosa
Adelaide, SA, Australia   Nisreen Moosa
September 2018

CONTENTS

ABBREVIATIONS

ABC	Australian Broadcasting Corporation
ACFE	Association of Certified Fraud Examiners
AIDS	Acquired Immune Deficiency Syndrome
AT&T	American Telephone and Telegraph
BBC	British Broadcasting Corporation
BCBS	Basel Committee on Banking Supervision
BRICS	Brazil, Russia, India, China and South Africa
CA	California
CEO	Chief Executive Officer
CGD	Center for Global Development
CIA	Central Intelligence Agency
CIGI	Centre for International Governance Innovation
CNY	Chinese yuan
COSATU	Congress of South African Trade Unions
CPI	Corruption Perception Index
CRA	Contingent Reserve Arrangement
DC	District of Columbia
EU	European Union
EUR	Euro
FBI	Federal Bureau of Investigation
FCIC	Financial Crisis Inquiry Commission
FDI	Foreign Direct Investment
FDIC	Federal Deposit Insurance Corporation
GAO	Government Accountability Office
GBP	British pound
GDP	Gross Domestic Product
HIV	Human Immunodeficiency Virus

HQ	Headquarters
IBRD	International Bank for Reconstruction and Development
IEO	Independent Evaluation Office
IMF	International Monetary Fund
IMFC	International Monetary and Financial Committee
IPES	International Political Economy Society
JPY	Japanese yen
KBR	Kellogg Brown & Root
LDC	Less Developed Country
MIT	Massachusetts Institute of Technology
MNC	Multinational Corporation
MP	Member of Parliament
NBER	National Bureau of Economic Research
NSA	National Security Agency
OTC	Over the Counter
PA	Pennsylvania
PIGS	Portugal, Ireland, Greece and Spain
PR	Public Relations
PRGF	Poverty Reduction and Growth Facility
R&D	Research and Development
S&L	Savings and Loan
SAP	Structural Adjustment Programme
SBS	Special Broadcasting Service
SDR	Special Drawing Rights
SEC	Securities and Exchange Commission
SIFI	Systemically Important Financial Institution
TB	Tuberculosis
TBTF	Too Big to Fail
TX	Texas
UN	United Nations
UNCTAD	United Nations Conference on Trade and Development
UNISA	University of South Australia
UNITA	National Union for the Total Independence of Angola
USD	US dollar
VA	Virginia
WP	Working Paper

List of Figures

LIST OF TABLES

CHAPTER 1

The IMF at Face Value

1.1 Introduction

The International Monetary Fund (IMF), also known as the Fund, was established in July 1944 as a product of a conference that was held in Bretton Woods (New Hampshire, US) to formulate and implement monetary arrangements, pertaining to exchange rates and international payment mechanisms, for the post-war period. Exchange rate arrangements were the prime focus of the 44 participating countries in view of the damage inflicted on the world economy by competitive devaluation and the extensive use of *beggar-thy-neighbour* policies in the 1930s. Those policies contributed to the intensification of the Great Depression and led to dwindling international trade. In essence, the primary function of the IMF was set to be the supervision of the Bretton Woods system of fixed but adjustable exchange rates.

In 2012, however, the Fund's mandate was upgraded to give it more responsibilities encompassing issues that pertain to international macroeconomic and financial stability. This may sound peculiar, given that the Bretton Woods system of fixed but adjustable exchange rates collapsed in 1971 following the announcement by President Richard Nixon of the decision to abolish the convertibility of the dollar into gold, which was one of the main pillars of the system. By 1978, and following years of drifting towards floating, a new international monetary system emerged whereby countries are allowed to adopt the exchange rate systems that they deem suitable for their economies. Hence the extended IMF mandate

© The Author(s) 2019
I. A. Moosa, N. Moosa, *Eliminating the IMF*,
https://doi.org/10.1007/978-3-030-05761-9_1

must have been in place long before 2012—otherwise, the Fund would have had nothing to do in the absence of a system that it was created to supervise. Currently, this is how the IMF describes its responsibilities in the factsheets posted on its website:

> The International Monetary Fund, or IMF, promotes international financial stability and monetary cooperation. It also facilitates international trade, promotes employment and sustainable economic growth, and helps to reduce global poverty.

In a way, therefore, the IMF has turned itself into many things, including a financial and macroeconomic advisor, a trade promoter and a development agency. These functions are invariably performed and the underlying responsibilities assumed by other international organisations, including the Bank for International Settlements, the World Trade Organisation (the United Nations Conference on Trade and Development [UNCTAD] before that) and the World Bank.

The objective of this chapter is to present an overview of how the IMF perceives itself, particularly with respect to its responsibilities and accomplishments. We present a description of these responsibilities and accomplishments as portrayed by the IMF—hence it is a portrayal of the IMF at "face value". We start by examining the origin and growth of the IMF. An account of the international monetary systems in operation before and after the establishment of the IMF is presented in Sect. 1.8.

1.2   Origin and Growth

The 1944 Bretton Woods conference materialised as a result of the work of John Maynard Keynes (then of the British Treasury) and Harry Dexter White, of the US Treasury, on the development of ideas pertaining to the post-war international monetary system. H.D. White believed that the IMF should function like a bank, making sure that borrowers would not default and meet their repayments on time. J.M. Keynes, on the other hand, was in favour of the idea that the IMF would be a cooperative fund upon which member states could draw to maintain economic activity and employment through periodic crises. The view of H.D. White prevailed, eventually leading to the use of conditionality provisions to make sure that borrowing countries repay their debt.

Following negotiations, mainly between British and American officials, a "Joint Statement by Experts on the Establishment of an International Monetary Fund" was published simultaneously in a number of Allied countries on 21 April 1944. In the following month, the US government invited the representatives of 44 countries to participate in a conference that was held in the Mount Washington Hotel in Bretton Woods, New Hampshire, to discuss a framework for a post-war international monetary system. The conference became known as the "Bretton Woods Conference" or, more formally, "the United Nations Monetary and Financial Conference". A total of 730 delegates participated in the conference over the period 1–22 July 1944. Schuler and Bernkopf (2014) provide a "nearly complete list" of the people who attended the conference by collating published documents containing lists of participants.

The main products of the Bretton Woods conference were (i) articles of agreement for the establishment of the IMF to supervise exchange rate arrangements; (ii) articles of agreement for the establishment of the International Bank for Reconstruction and Development (IBRD), which subsequently became the World Bank, to supervise post-war reconstruction and foster economic development; and (iii) other recommendations and thoughts pertaining to international economic cooperation. The IMF agreement comprised the following components: (i) an exchange rate system of fixed but adjustable exchange rates whereby adjustment is resorted to only to correct a "fundamental disequilibrium"; (ii) currency convertibility for the purpose of settling current account transactions; and (iii) subscription to the IMF's capital (the quota system). The articles of agreement for the IMF signed at Bretton Woods did not come into force until its ratification by countries commanding at least 80% of capital subscriptions—that threshold was reached on 27 December 1945 with the participation of 29 countries.

The IMF was organised formally in a meeting held in Savannah, Georgia, during the period 8–18 March 1946. By the end of 1946 the IMF had grown to 39 members, and on 1 March 1947, the Fund began its financial operations when France became the first borrower on 8 May of that year. Because of the damage inflicted on Europe in World War II, the Bretton Woods agreement allowed for inconvertibility of the currencies of European countries while they were rebuilding their economies. It was not until the late 1950s that European currencies became convertible again. The Japanese yen (JPY) did not become convertible until the early 1960s.

The IMF's influence was enhanced by the growth of membership as more and more countries joined the Fund following their independence from colonial powers. It is noteworthy, however, that not all member countries of the IMF are sovereign states, in the sense of being members of the United Nations (UN). Examples are non-sovereign regions that are officially under the sovereignty of full UN member states, such as Aruba, Curaçao, Hong Kong and Macau. Former members include Cuba (left in 1964) and Taiwan, which in 1980 was replaced as a member of the UN by the People's Republic of China. However, the IMF recognises the "Taiwan Province of China", at least for statistical purposes. Apart from Cuba, other UN members that are not members of the IMF include Andorra, Liechtenstein, Monaco and North Korea. The former Czechoslovakia was expelled in 1954 for failing to provide the data required by the IMF, which is a condition of membership, but it was readmitted in 1990 following the collapse of the Soviet Union. Poland withdrew from the IMF in 1950 but resumed membership in 1986.

To qualify for IMF membership, a country must (i) make periodic membership payments towards their quotas, (ii) refrain from currency restrictions unless granted IMF permission, (iii) abide by the code of conduct in the IMF articles of agreement and (iv) provide national economic data and information. During the period between 1945 and 1971, when the Bretton Woods system was in operation, member countries agreed to maintain their exchange rates at levels that could be adjusted only to correct a "fundamental disequilibrium" in the balance of payments, and only with the IMF's approval. According to the IMF, the benefits of membership include (i) access to information on the economic policies of all member countries; (ii) the opportunity to influence other members' economic policies; (iii) technical assistance in banking, fiscal affairs and exchange matters; (iv) financial support for countries experiencing payment difficulties; and (v) increased opportunities for trade and investment (see, e.g., https://www.imf.org/external/np/exr/center/mm/eng/mm_bnfts.htm).

1.3   SURVEILLANCE

Surveillance is a formal system used by the IMF to monitor economic policies and indicators on national, regional and global levels, with the objective of maintaining stability and avoiding crises. By monitoring economic and financial developments, the IMF is in a position to provide advice to member countries and promote policies. According to the IMF's website, the Fund supports policies that "foster economic stability, reduce vulner-ability to economic and financial crises, and raise living standards". Surveillance is believed to be important for the purpose of "identifying stability and growth risks that may require remedial policy adjustments". The IMF describes "vigilant monitoring" as "critical" because "the prob-lems or policies of one country can affect many others".

The function of surveillance involves annual visits to member countries to enable the IMF staff to meet government and central bank officials for the purpose of conducting discussions about exchange rates, monetary policy, fiscal policy and regulatory policy, as well as "structural reforms". The visits also involve meetings with members of the legislature and rep-resentatives from the business community, labour unions and civil society. The results of the discussions are presented in a report to the Executive Board, which subsequently transmits the findings and recommendations to the country in question as part of what is known as "Article IV consul-tation". The country may issue a press release summarising the analysis and recommendations coming out of the exercise.

A product of the function of surveillance is a set of reports, including *World Economic Outlook, Global Financial Stability Report, Fiscal Monitor* and *External Sector Report*, as well as a series of regional economic out-looks. The *World Economic Outlook* provides analysis of the global econ-omy and its growth prospects, dealing with issues such as the macroeconomic effects of global financial turmoil and the potential for global spillovers. The *Global Financial Stability Report* monitors financial imbalances and vulnerabilities that pose potential risks to financial stability. The *Fiscal Monitor* updates medium-term fiscal projections and assesses the state of public finance in member countries (government revenue, expenditure and fiscal balances). *External Sector Reports* analyse and assess the external positions of the world's largest economies. The analysis presents a system-atic assessment of current accounts, exchange rates, external balance sheet positions, capital flows and international reserves. Twice a year the IMF issues a *Global Policy Agenda* that pulls together the key findings of and policy advice derived from various reports, proposing a future policy agenda for the IMF and its members.

The IMF periodically reviews its surveillance and monitoring activities as the global economy changes and crises erupt. The 2011 review focused on multilateral surveillance, laying the foundation for the 2012 Integrated Surveillance Decision, which focuses on domestic and balance of payments stability, as well as systemic stability. In September 2012 the Financial

Surveillance Strategy was endorsed to strengthen IMF monitoring. The 2014 review recognised the need to make surveillance adaptable, emphasising selectivity. A key priority was to fine-tune surveillance through better tailoring of advice on the fiscal, monetary, external and structural policy mix, based on cross-country experiences and supported by a more client-focused approach. Five operational priorities were identified for the period 2014–2019: risks and spillovers, macro-financial surveillance, structural policy advice, cohesive and expert policy advice, and a client-focused approach.

1.4   FINANCIAL ASSISTANCE

The IMF provides loans to member countries for the purpose of dealing with actual or potential balance of payments difficulties. The financing function is typically a component of an adjustment programme that is designed "in close cooperation with the IMF". In April 2009, in the aftermath of the global financial crisis, the IMF "strengthened its lending capacity and approved a major overhaul of its financial support mechanisms". A change was introduced in 2009 to boost the loan resources available to low-income countries such that the average limits under the IMF's concessional loan facilities were doubled. In 2016 the limits under non-concessional lending facilities were reviewed and expanded. In addition, zero interest rates on concessional loans were extended through the end of 2018, whereas the interest rate on emergency financing is permanently set at zero. In 2014 loan resources were replenished to support the IMF's concessional lending.

The main source of financing for the loans granted by the IMF to member countries are the quotas assigned to member countries, which constitute contributions to the IMF capital. These quotas, which are based on the relative positions in the world economy, are reviewed regularly. A formula is used to determine the quotas by considering as primary determining variables the size of the economy (measured in terms of gross domestic product [GDP]) and the level of openness (with weights of 0.5 and 0.3, respectively).

The quotas determine resource contributions (the maximum amount of financial resources provided by a member country) and voting power (such that one vote is equal to SDR100,000), which means that the total number of votes for a country is its quota divided by 100,000. Figure 1.1 shows the percentage of quotas of the top 20 countries, with the US appearing on top (as expected) whereas Indonesia is number 20. The pattern of the corresponding votes is exactly identical.

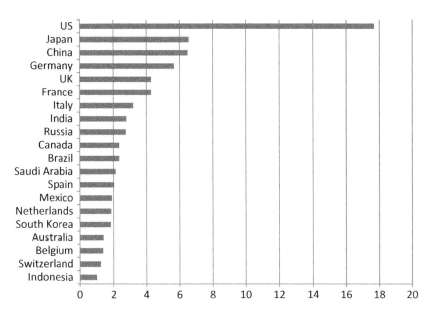

Fig. 1.1   IMF quotas (%)

1.5   Capacity Development

The IMF provides technical assistance and training with the objective of helping member countries to "build better economic institutions and strengthen related human capacities". Technical assistance and training cover a number of areas including policy design, regulation and supervision, legislation and economic statistics. As far as fiscal policy is concerned, the objective is to "enable governments to maintain fiscal sustainability, enhance infrastructure (such as schools, roads and hospitals), improve social safety nets, and attract greater investments". The areas covered under fiscal policy include the mobilisation of revenues, management of public expenditure, budget formulation, management of domestic and foreign debt, and the establishment of social safety nets. With respect to monetary policy, the objective is to help central banks pursue sound monetary and exchange rate policies. The Fund also works with financial regulators in member countries to boost financial regulation and supervision, with the objective of establishing macroeconomic and financial stability. With respect to the legal framework, the objective is to align the legal and governance frameworks to the international standards designed to fight corruption and combat money laundering. The Fund also helps member countries to do a good job of compiling, managing and reporting macroeconomic and financial data.

According to the IMF's website, the Fund's capacity development work is helping member countries in their efforts to reduce inequality (by implementing inclusive policies such as expenditure and subsidy reform, progressive taxation and financial inclusion), promote gender equality (by enabling countries to understand the impact of their economic policies on women and boost female labour market participation) and address climate action (by using environmental tax reform and efficient energy pricing to minimise the effects of climate change).

1.6   Special Drawing Rights

Special Drawing Rights (SDR) represent an international reserve asset issued by the IMF for the purpose of supplementing the official reserves of member countries. The collapse of the Bretton Woods system and the consequent resort to floating exchange rates have reduced the need to rely on the SDR as an international reserve asset. However, SDR allocations still play a role in providing liquidity and supplementing member countries' official reserves. The SDR is also used as the unit of account of the IMF and some other international organisations.

Under the Bretton Woods system, the value of the SDR was initially set at 0.888671 grammes of fine gold, making it equivalent to US $1. After the collapse of Bretton Woods, the SDR was redefined as a basket of currencies, which is a formula expressing the exchange rate of the SDR against the dollar in terms of the dollar exchange rates of major currencies. Initially, "major currencies" included the euro (EUR) (and before that it was the German mark), Japanese yen and pound. In November 2015 the Board of Governors decided that the Chinese yuan (CNY) met the criteria for inclusion in the SDR basket, becoming a component of the basket on 1 October 2016.

The SDR value in terms of the US dollar (USD) (i.e., the exchange rate between the SDR and USD) is determined on a daily basis, by observing the spot exchange rates of major currencies at noon London time, and posted on the IMF website. The exchange rate against the dollar is the sum of the dollar equivalent of predetermined currency amounts. Table 1.1 shows an example of how the SDR exchange rate is calculated, which gives a USD/SDR rate of 1.42—that is, each SDR is

Table 1.1 An example of the SDR exchange rate calculation

Currency	Currency amount	Exchange rate	Dollar equivalent	Implied weight (%)
USD	0.5825	1.0000	0.5825	41.11
EUR	0.3867	1.1628	0.4497	31.74
GBP	0.0859	1.3699	0.1177	8.31
CNY	1.0174	0.1560	0.1587	11.20
JPY	11.9000	0.0091	0.1083	7.64
		USD/SDR	1.4169	100.00

worth $1.4169. The exchange rate can be expressed as SDR/USD, which is the price of one dollar in terms of the SDR by inverting the USD/SDR rate to arrive at 0.7058. The dollar equivalent amount is the product of the currency amount by the exchange rate. The implied weight of the currency is the currency amount multiplied by the ratio of the USD/SDR rate to the USD rate of the underlying currency.

The SDR basket, in terms of both the component currencies and their weights, is reviewed every five years and changed if necessary to reflect the relative importance of each currency in international trade and the global financial system. The currency amounts remain fixed over the five-year period but the actual weights of currencies in the basket fluctuate with changes in the cross exchange rates among the basket currencies. Two main conditions must be met before a currency is included in the SDR basket: (i) the currency is issued by an IMF member, or a monetary union that includes IMF members, such that it is one of the top five exporters of the world; and (ii) the currency is widely used to settle international transactions and widely traded in the foreign exchange market.

The interest rate on the SDR is charged to members on their non-concessional borrowing from the IMF and paid to members for their remunerated creditor positions in the IMF. It is also the interest paid to members on their SDR holdings and charged on their SDR allocations. The interest rate is determined weekly as a weighted average of representative interest rates on short-term government debt instruments in the money markets of the basket currencies. Since the structure of the SDR basket is known publicly, the interest rate on the SDR can only be calculated as a weighted average of the interest rates of the component currencies (otherwise riskless arbitrage opportunities would arise).

1.7   Governance and Organisation

The IMF is accountable to its member country governments. At the top of its organisational structure is the Board of Governors, consisting of one governor and one alternate governor from each member country, usually a top official from the central bank or finance ministry. The Board of Governors meets once a year at the IMF-World Bank annual meetings. Twenty four governors serve on the International Monetary and Financial Committee, or IMFC, which provides advice to the Executive Board on the supervision and management of the international monetary and financial system. The managing director, who is assisted by four deputy managing directors, is the head of the IMF staff and chair of the Executive Board.

1.8   The International Monetary System Pre- and Post-IMF

In this section we review the international monetary system before and after the establishment of the IMF. We can identify a number of episodes, starting with the classical gold standard and finishing with the current system.

The Classical Gold Standard

Under the classical gold standard, exchange rates were determined by the fixed prices of gold in terms of each currency. The classical gold standard did not encompass the entire world but only a core of major countries led by Britain. Britain went on the gold standard in 1821, when the Bank of England was legally required to redeem its notes and coins in gold and when the prohibition of the melting of coins and export of gold was repealed. The system came to an abrupt end at the beginning of World War I in August 1914, when the warring countries abolished the convertibility of their currencies into gold and into each other. By the mid-1870s France had abandoned bimetallism (using both gold and silver as reserves) in favour of gold. In 1870 Germany was still on the silver standard, but war reparations in the form of gold payments from France enabled it to adopt the gold standard. And in 1879 the US returned to the gold standard after the suspension of gold convertibility during the Civil War. In general, 1870 is regarded as the year in which the gold standard became internationally operational.

The Inter-War Period

In the period between the end of World War I and 1926, a system of flexible exchange rates was adopted. The desire to go back to the gold standard could not be fulfilled because of a shortage of gold at the pre-war levels of the fixed exchange rates. In 1922 the Genoa Conference recommended worldwide adoption of a gold exchange standard, whereby the pound would be convertible into gold and other currencies would be convertible into pounds. The gold exchange standard was born in 1925 when Britain re-established the convertibility of the pound into gold. The system came to an end when in 1931 the French decided not to accept any more pounds and to exchange their holdings of the British currency for gold. There was little that Britain could do other than to make the pound inconvertible into gold. The ensuing period witnessed the Great Depression (1931–1939) and open economic warfare conducted mainly via competitive devaluation.

The inter-war experiment with the gold exchange standard failed because the world economy had experienced significant changes as a result of war and the Great Depression. Those events rendered the pre-war exchange rates inappropriate because of widely divergent inflation rates, which provided the impetus for developing the theory of purchasing power parity in its modern form by Gustav Cassel (e.g., Cassel 1916). Furthermore, prices and wages became rigid (particularly downwards), hindering the establishment of equilibrium. More importantly perhaps is that countries did not follow the "rules of the game" because of concern about domestic economic instability.

The Bretton Woods System

Negotiators at Bretton Woods sought an exchange rate system that would combine the advantages of both fixed and flexible exchange rates (perhaps too good to be true). The choice was a system of fixed but adjustable exchange rates, the adjustable peg. Accordingly, the dollar was pegged to gold at the fixed price of $35/ounce and the US stood ready to buy and sell unlimited amounts of the metal at this price. Other countries were required to declare the exchange rates of their currencies against the dollar and to defend the declared rates in the foreign exchange market by buying and selling dollars (hence the dollar was the intervention currency). Exchange rates could only vary within the intervention points, initially fixed at ±1% around the declared par values (the fixed rates).

The Bretton Woods system suffered from a number of problems that led to its eventual demise. The first problem pertains to the adjustment mechanism (of the balance of payments). The system lacked a real adjustment mechanism as governments had to demonstrate the existence of a fundamental disequilibrium in the balance of payments before they could adjust their exchange rates. The system lacked the stability, certainty and automaticity of the gold standard and the flexibility of free floating. Under the Bretton Woods system, speculation in the foreign exchange market was extremely destabilising because of the possibility of changing the fixed rates through devaluation or revaluation. A currency under pressure (perhaps because the country concerned was running out of reserves) could only be devalued, motivating speculators to sell or short sell that currency.

An important loophole in the system was the defects in the liquidity creation mechanism, leading to the emergence of the vicious circle of the "Triffin Dilemma" or "Triffin Paradox" (after Robert Triffin, the economist who first recognised the problem). To avoid a liquidity shortage, the US had to run a balance of payments deficit, thus undermining confidence in the dollar. To avoid speculation against the dollar, the deficit had to shrink, leading to a liquidity shortage. One solution to this problem was suggested in 1968, which was the creation of SDR as an international currency.

The Bretton Woods era can be divided into two periods: (i) period of dollar shortage, 1944–1958 and (ii) period of dollar glut, 1958–1971. The second period was characterised by a significant US balance of payments deficit at a time when surplus countries (Germany and Japan) were resisting the revaluation of their currencies. In 1962 France began to exchange dollars for gold, which led other countries to worry about whether sufficient amounts of gold would remain for them after the French had finished exchanging their dollars. Feeling the pressure, the US became severely constrained, particularly by the fact that it was unable to change its exchange rate. On 15 August 1971 the US government responded to a record $30 billion trade deficit by making the dollar inconvertible into gold, as announced by President Richard Nixon. This action, similar to the action taken by Britain in 1931, marked the collapse of the Bretton Woods system.

The Present System

On 18 December 1971 the ten major industrial countries tried to salvage the Bretton Woods system by signing the Smithsonian Agreement in Washington, DC. The US agreed to raise the official price of gold to $38/ ounce but refused to restore the free convertibility of the dollar into gold. Other countries, in return, agreed to revalue their currencies against the dollar. Moreover, exchange rates were allowed to fluctuate within a wider band of ±2.5%.

This agreement, however, did not solve any of the fundamental defects of the Bretton Woods system. As a result, floating became widespread in 1973, while European countries experimented with the "Snake in the Tunnel" as a system of fixed exchange rates. The floating exchange rate system was not legalised until January 1976 when the Jamaica Accord was signed (with ratification coming in 1978). The accord allowed countries the freedom of choice of the exchange rate system they deemed appropriate for their economies, encouraging them not to resort to competitive devaluation. There was also an agreement to pursue domestic economic policies that are conducive to stability. The official price of gold was abolished, allowing it to fluctuate according to market forces.

Currently, major industrial countries adopt a system of floating exchange rates, while a number of European countries have adopted a single currency, the euro. The current system has failed in three major areas. The first is exchange rate misalignment (deviations of exchange rates from their "fair values"). The second area is that the system has failed to deliver policy autonomy, in the sense of cutting policy links among countries. The consequence of these links is that economic policy in one country, particularly if it is a major country, leads to effects that are transmitted abroad. The third is protectionism, resulting from exchange rate misalignment and the distortion of international competitive positions.

The Jamaica Accord gave countries the freedom of choosing the arrangements they deemed appropriate for their economies. Not all countries opted for floating: some chose other systems encompassing a spectrum with respect to exchange rate flexibility. This is why these arrangements are sometimes described as being "eclectic". The Appendix provides a description of the exchange rate systems used by one or more countries under the present system.

1.9   Concluding Remarks

In this chapter we presented a self-portrayal of the IMF, but not everyone sees the IMF this way. Rickards (2016) describes the Washington area as "thick with secret agencies with three-letter names, such as CIA, FBI, NSA". Yet he believes that "one of the most powerful, and also most secretive, of these agencies is an institution that is not even part of the U.S. government"—by that he means the IMF. He describes the IMF as "an autonomous part of an emerging scheme of global governance accountable only to a small elite of central bankers, finance ministers and heads of state". With respect to secrecy, this is what he has to say:

> The IMF has a convoluted governance structure in which the highest decision-making body, the Board of Governors, has little power because the votes are weighted in favor of the largest economies, such as the U.S. Actual power rests with the blandly named International Monetary and Financial Committee, the IMFC. Everything about the IMF is designed to make it difficult for outsiders like you to have any idea what is going on. The insiders like that arrangement just fine.

With reference to the book *Money and Tough Love: On Tour with the IMF*, by Ahamed (2014), Richards talks about "IMF missions as they monitor large and small governments around the world", suggesting that "these missions are the key to forcing governments to conform to the rules of the game as established by the global monetary elites". The book describes how the Fund goes about its business on a day-to-day basis, and how it has "the power to make or break sovereign governments by deciding whether or not to make loans when those governments are in financial distress". It is suggested that the IMF is just as powerful as the military and Central Intelligence Agency (CIA) when it comes to forcing regime change in governments that do not follow US orders. For this purpose, the IMF uses the weapon of money as effectively as when the military uses special operations or the CIA uses drones.

Most of the world does not see the IMF as the Fund sees itself. The views expressed by Rickards (2016) are just the tip of the iceberg, as we will find out by going on a discovery of the alternative views of the IMF. Currently three views represent the attitude towards the IMF. First is the view that with the collapse of the Bretton Woods system, the IMF is no longer needed and that it should be abolished. The second view is that the IMF is still vital, but needs to be restructured and refocused. The most positive view of the IMF is that new functions should be added to it and that its role in the international monetary system should be expanded.

Appendix: Taxonomy of Exchange Rate Arrangements

At one time the IMF was in charge of supervising one predominant system of fixed exchange rates. Currently, the Fund cannot tell member countries what exchange rate system to adopt, as this would contravene the Jamaica Accord. Rather, the Fund reports the exchange rate arrangements followed by each member country, which is obliged to inform the IMF of any change in its exchange rate arrangement. The problem here is that countries do not necessarily practise what they declare, in the sense that the actual exchange rate arrangement they follow is not the same as the declared one. This has led to the emergence of a strand of the literature dealing with exchange rate regime verification, distinguishing between de facto and de jure regimes (for details, see Moosa 2005). For example, in July 2005, China declared that it was moving from a single peg to a basket peg but, at least in the immediate period, the exchange rate of the yuan behaved more like a crawling peg (see, e.g., Moosa et al. 2009; Moosa and Li 2017). The following are the exchange rate regimes used under the present system of "national preference".

Exchange Arrangements with No Separate Legal Tender

Under this arrangement, the currency of another country circulates as the sole legal tender. Alternatively, the country belongs to a monetary or currency union in which the same legal tender is shared by members of the union. This includes the countries using the euro and members of other currency unions (e.g., Grenada is part of the East Caribbean Currency Union).

Currency Board

A currency board is an arrangement that is based on an explicit legislative commitment to exchange the domestic currency for a specified foreign currency at a fixed exchange rate, combined with restrictions on the issuing authority to ensure the fulfilment of its legal obligation.

Other Conventional Fixed Peg Arrangements

These arrangements include pegging to a single currency and pegging to a basket of currencies, such as the SDR. Under these arrangements, the country pegs its currency (formally or de facto) at a fixed rate to a single currency or a basket of currencies, allowing the actual exchange rate to fluctuate within a narrow margin of less than ±1% around a central rate (the rate determined by the arrangement).

Pegged Exchange Rates with Horizontal Bands

This arrangement is similar to the previous one, except that the band within which the exchange rate is allowed to fluctuate is wider than ±1%.

Crawling Peg

Under a crawling peg, the exchange rate is adjusted periodically at a fixed, pre-announced small rate or in response to changes in some quantitative indicators (e.g., inflation).

Exchange Rates with Crawling Bands

An arrangement of crawling bands requires the exchange rate to be maintained within a certain band around a central rate that is adjusted periodically at a fixed, pre-announced rate or in response to changes in some indicators.

Managed Floating with No Pre-announced Path for the Exchange Rate

Under this arrangement, the exchange rate is determined by market forces but the monetary authority intervenes actively in the foreign exchange market without specifying a path for the exchange rate.

Independent Floating

Under independent floating the exchange rate is determined by market forces. Any intervention in the foreign exchange market aims at curbing exchange rate volatility.

References

Ahamed, L. (2014). *Money and Tough Love: On Tour with the IMF.* London: Visual Editions.

Cassel, G. (1916). The Present Situation of the Foreign Exchange. *Economic Journal, 26,* 62–65.

Moosa, I. A. (2005). *Exchange Rate Regimes: Fixed, Flexible or Something in Between?* London: Palgrave.

Moosa, I. A., & Li, L. (2017). The Mystery of the Chinese Exchange Rate Regime: Basket or No Basket? *Applied Economics, 49,* 349–360.

Moosa, I. A., Naughton, A., & Li, L. (2009). Exchange Rate Regime Verification: Has China Actually Moved from a Dollar Peg to a Basket Peg? *Economia Internazionale, 62,* 41–67.

Rickards, J. (2016, August 4). Behind the Scenes of the Monetary Agency That Is Just as Powerful as the Military and CIA. *The Daily Reckoning.* http://www.businessinsider.com/the-imf-is-just-as-powerful-as-the-military-and-cia-2016-8?IR=T

Schuler, K., & Bernkopf, M. (2014, July). Who Was at Bretton Woods? Center for Financial Stability, Papers in Financial History. http://www.centerforfinancial-stability.org/bw/Who_Was_at_Bretton_Woods.pdf

CHAPTER 2

The Washington Consensus

2.1 THE TEN COMMANDMENTS

The Washington Consensus, a term that was coined by Williamson (1989), is a set of ten policy prescriptions promoted by institutions based in Washington, DC—primarily, the International Monetary Fund (IMF), the World Bank and the US Treasury—and by the governments of free market-loving "western" countries. The Consensus is associated with neoliberal policies in general, embodying a desire to let the almighty market call the shots while encouraging a diminishing role for the government in economic activity. On an international level, the philosophy behind the Washington Consensus is used to justify globalisation and US hegemony. We shall use the term "ten commandments" to refer to the ten policy prescriptions comprising the Consensus and the term "Washington preachers" to refer to the individuals, institutions and countries that preach the ten commandments. Ironically, developing countries are preached and advised to follow the ten commandments, on the grounds that they lead to prosperity, while the preaching countries (most notably the US) do not follow the commandments themselves. It is a clear case of preaching without doing and the opposite of leading by example.

Rodrik (2006) describes the Consensus as "stabilize, privatize, and liberalize", which became the mantra of a generation of technocrats, who cut their teeth in the developing world, and of the political leaders they counselled. While Rodrik is right in arguing that the Consensus involves privatisation and liberalisation, he is wrong about "stabilisation". Justifying

© The Author(s) 2019
I. A. Moosa, N. Moosa, *Eliminating the IMF*,
https://doi.org/10.1007/978-3-030-05761-9_2

privatisation and liberalisation is easier under unstable conditions—the argument then would be that privatisation and liberalisation are needed for the purpose of stabilisation. Rodrik points out that while China and India have made their economies reliant on free-market forces to a limited extent, their general economic policies remained the exact opposite to the main recommendations of the Washington Consensus. Had they been dismal failures, they would have presented strong evidence in support of the ten commandments, but that was not to be the case as they turned out to be case studies of successful economic development. According to Rodrik, "while the lessons drawn by proponents and skeptics differ, it is fair to say that nobody really believes in the Washington Consensus anymore". The question now, he argues, "is not whether the Washington Consensus is dead or alive; it is what will replace it".

In what follows, the ten commandments are discussed in turn. It will be demonstrated that the commandments are not followed by the Washington preachers themselves and that the economic rationale behind them is rather weak. The ten commandments do not necessarily lead to prosperity and their blanket application to countries of all sorts could bring about disastrous effects.

2.2   The First Commandment: Fiscal Policy Discipline

The objective behind the policy recommendation of fiscal discipline is to avoid large fiscal deficits relative to gross domestic product (GDP). This commandment is based on the concept of a "fiscal straitjacket", requiring the placement of strict constraints on government spending and public sector borrowing, with the objective of keeping the lid on the budget deficit. On the surface, this is fine as fiscal profligacy can be deadly, but this policy prescription should not be taken at face value and accepted without scrutiny. The first observation is that nothing is said about the distribution of government spending, in which case this objective may be achieved by cutting social expenditure on health and education without touching (or even while boosting) military expenditure, which is the least productive. This is what we observe today in the US, the UK and Australia, among other countries. The other problem is that the Washington preachers, "western" countries, typically indulge in fiscal profligacy—most notably the US. The rest of this section is devoted to a discussion of the US deficit, which shows that this country, which is where the IMF resides, is the biggest violator of the first commandment.

The US budget deficit has been recognised as a major problem that threatens the long-term prospects of the US economy, and yet nothing is being done about it—on the contrary it is worsening as military expenditure grows for the benefit of war profiteers. In a June 2010 opinion piece in the *Wall Street Journal*, the former chairman of the Federal Reserve, Alan Greenspan, noted that "only politically toxic cuts or rationing of medical care, a marked rise in the eligible age for health and retirement benefits, or significant inflation, can close the deficit" (Greenspan 2010). He warned that "if significant reforms are not undertaken, benefits under entitlement programs will exceed government income by over $40 trillion over the next 75 years". Kotlikoff (2006) argues that the US "must eventually choose between bankruptcy, raising taxes, or cutting payouts". In general he points out that "countries can go broke, the United States is going broke, that remaining open to foreign investment can help stave off bankruptcy, but that radical reform of US fiscal institutions is essential to secure the nation's economic future". He offers three policies to eliminate the fiscal gap and avert bankruptcy: (i) a federal retail sales tax, (ii) personalised social security and (iii) a globally budgeted universal healthcare system. It is ironic that the major "fiscal institution" referred to by Kotlikoff is the US Treasury, one of the custodians of the Washington Consensus that preaches fiscal discipline to the rest of the world.

Warnings about the prospects of an uncontrollable budget deficit and the consequences for public debt have become quite common. For example, a report of the Peter Peterson Foundation (2010) states the following:

> The US faces a looming fiscal crisis. With escalating deficits, mounting levels of public debt, growing unfunded promises for large individual, entitlement programs, and increasing reliance on foreign lenders, we as US citizens should be very concerned about the deteriorating financial conditions of our nation.

The problem with the US deficit is that it is not just a passing phenomenon—rather it is a structural long-term problem created by addiction to excessive spending and the belief that tax cuts pay for themselves. The Peter Peterson Foundation (2010) describes the situation as follows:

The deficits for fiscal years 2009 and 2010 are largely attributable to significant declines in revenue due to a recession and weak economy, the cost of the wars in Iraq and Afghanistan, and various government bailouts and stimulus actions. These items do not represent long-term and recurring fiscal challenges. However, even after the economy recovers, the special federal interventions are complete, the wars are over, and unemployment levels are down, deficits and debt are expected to grow at a rapid rate. As a result, the US will find itself in an unsustainable fiscal position in the years to come. If current policies are left unchanged, debt held by the public is projected to spike even further, reaching over 300 percent of GDP in 2040.

According to the Peter Peterson Foundation (2010), a big threat comes from interest payments, which are projected to be "the largest single line item in the federal budget—larger than defense, Medicare or Social Security". Assuming that the US does not have to pay a risk premium, it is estimated that by 2040, federal interest costs will account for 14% of GDP. If interest rates rise just two percentage points, interest costs alone could represent about 20% of GDP by 2040. The estimates show that by 2024, historical revenue levels of about 18% of GDP will not cover interest payments, social security, Medicare and Medicaid. This means that the US government will need to borrow to pay for other essential programmes such as education, transport and everything else that keeps the economy going. The dismal conclusion of the report of the Peter Peterson Foundation is that:

> If we continue down this path, rising deficit and debt levels will impact our everyday lives by threatening our nation's economic strength (lower investment and growth), our international status (weaker standing in the world and international capital markets), our standard of living (higher interest rates for loans and mortgages, higher unemployment rates, lower wages), and possibly our national security (higher dependency on foreign governments that purchase US debt). Moreover, higher debt levels mean more resources devoted to compounding interest payments on the debt, which increasingly go abroad rather than stay in this country. Thus, we have fewer resources available for domestic investment in research and development, education, infrastructure and other crucial investments that maintain our economic competitiveness.

Yet nothing is being done about the problem. Samuelson (2009) argues that "the president does not want to confront Americans with choices between lower spending and higher taxes". The deficit problem cannot be solved with only spending cuts or higher taxes. Elements of a comprehensive solution may include, according to the Peter Peterson Foundation (2010), the reduction of military spending to pre-war levels, implementation of Department of Defense reforms, reviewing weapons systems, making procurement programmes more efficient, making military compensation and benefits more affordable, and reviewing and eliminating other ineffective programmes. Hence the underlying belief of the authors of the report is that excessive military spending is indeed a big problem that must be solved to get the budget deficit under control.

One has to be fair and say that under Trump, the US government is trying hard to reduce expenditure and the fiscal deficit—the question is how this is being done. In a brilliant speech (probably the best speech since Martin Luther King's "I have a dream"), Chris Hedges spelled out the numbers. Expenditure is being cut drastically over a period of ten years as follows: $9.2 billion from the Department of Education, $616 billion from Medicaid and the Children's Health Insurance Program, $200 billion from the food stamp programme (a lifeline for 44 million people who would otherwise starve), $39 billion from subsidised new loans and $850 million from the public sector loan forgiveness programme. Simultaneously, the Pentagon's budget was increased by half a trillion dollars over ten years. This is what Chris Hedges (2017) calls "acceleration of austerity and militarism".

The major preacher of the Washington Consensus seems to be the biggest violator of the first commandment. In Fig. 2.1 we observe the US federal debt and fiscal balance as a percentage of GDP. These figures indicate fiscal profligacy rather than discipline. Figure 2.2 displays recent numbers for the budget deficit as a percentage of GDP in a number of countries. It seems that Nicaragua, North Korea and Somalia are more fiscally disciplined than the UK and the US. In Fig. 2.3 we can see public debt as a percentage of GDP in a number of countries. The top seven are "western" countries (for some reason, Japan is sometimes classified as a "western" country, although, like Australia, it is located in the Far East). Here we have Nigeria, Congo and Afghanistan as more fiscally disciplined than the US. Is it not ludicrous that the IMF tells Nigeria, Congo and Afghanistan to behave themselves and show some fiscal discipline?

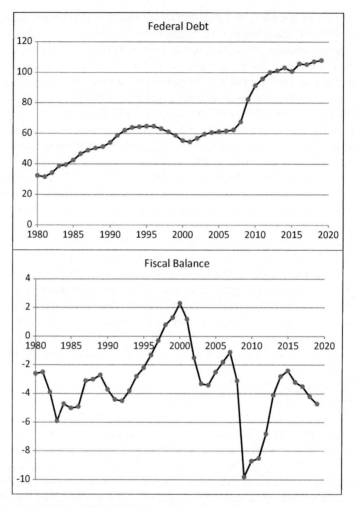

Fig. 2.1 US federal debt and fiscal deficit as a percentage of GDP

2.3   The Second Commandment: Redirection
of Public Spending

The second commandment involves the redirection of public expenditure away from subsidies (particularly indiscriminate subsidies) towards broad-based provision of key services like primary education, primary healthcare

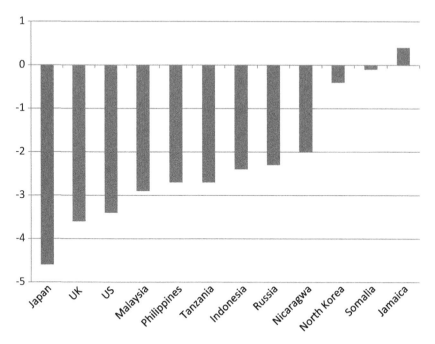

Fig. 2.2 Budget deficit as a percentage of GDP

and infrastructure. The rationale is that these areas are pro-poor and pro-growth, which sounds good.

Again, this policy prescription does not stand up to scrutiny. To start with, and as mentioned earlier, nothing is said about military spending, which is wasteful, but any cuts in military spending is bad for countries and companies exporting arms, most notably the UK and the US. More importantly perhaps is that the declared objective of boosting expenditure on health, education and infrastructure is counterfactual. In the countries preaching the second commandment, significant cuts of funding to health, education and infrastructure can be observed. Furthermore, IMF operations, which presumably follow this commandment, invariably lead to cuts in expenditure on health and education, as we are going to see in Chap. 5. IMF operations are intended mainly to make the borrowing countries capable of paying their debt to the IMF itself and to international bankers. Thus resources are diverted away from health and education to debt repayments. The austerity measures recommended by the IMF hurt the poor—this is not speculation but rather reality.

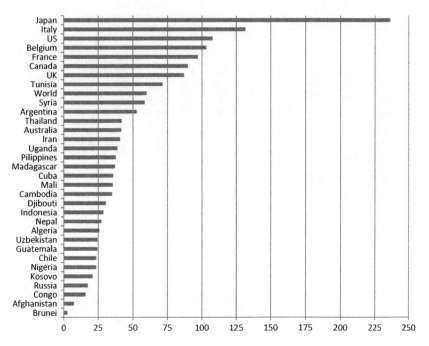

Fig. 2.3   Gross public debt as a percentage of GDP

2.4   THE THIRD COMMANDMENT: TAX REFORM

The declared objective with respect to tax reform is to achieve a broad tax base and adopt moderate marginal tax rates. Tax reform is the process of changing the way taxes are collected or managed by the government, with the objective of improving tax administration or to provide economic or social benefits. Tax reform may involve reduction of taxes for all people, making the tax system more progressive or less progressive, and simplifying the tax system by making it more understandable and more accountable.

The problem here is that the so-called tax reform, as practised in the preaching countries, is structured in such a way as to benefit the corporate sector and the rich at the expense of the poor. We often hear about proposals to reduce the corporate tax rate because the business sector creates jobs. We often hear that cutting taxes boosts economic growth, and that the process is self-funding as growth produces a higher level of government revenue. And we also often hear that cutting taxes for the rich is good for everyone because of the trickle-down effect. When applied to developing countries as recommended by the IMF, the objective of "tax reform" is to enable multinationals to get away with minimal tax payments, if any at all.

It may be worthwhile to say more about the trickle-down effect, which is used to justify poverty, inequality and the obscene amounts paid to the financial oligarchs and the Chief Executive Officers (CEOs) of private sector firms. The term "trickle down" originated in US politics, although it has been attributed to humourist Will Rogers, who said during the Great Depression that "money was all appropriated for the top in hopes that it would trickle down to the needy" (Sims and Boyle 2009; Giangreco and Moore 1999). In more recent history, the phrase is closely identified with critics of "Reaganomics". Ronald Reagan's budget director, David Stockman, was supportive of his boss's tax cuts at first, but subsequently he became critical of them. He told journalist William Greider that "supply-side economics is the trickle-down idea" and that "it's kind of hard to sell 'trickle down', so the supply-side formula was the only way to get a tax policy that was really 'trickle down'" (Greider 1981, 1982).

The underlying idea is that policies designed to benefit the wealthy, such as financial deregulation and favourable tax treatment of capital income, will "ultimately" benefit everybody. It is the proposition that the benefits of growth will "eventually" trickle down even to the poor or that "high tide carries all boats". This notion is similar to the idea of the "American dream"—that is, no one should worry about poverty because eventually beggars become billionaires. The twisted logic behind the trickle-down effect is that generously rewarding members of the upper 1% enhances productivity, leading to the provision of goods and services at a lower cost and to higher demand for the services of the common person who will therefore earn higher wages (eventually, of course).

The notion of trickle down has been criticised and ridiculed. In the 1992 presidential election, independent candidate Ross Perot called trickle-down economics "political voodoo". In New Zealand, Labour Party Member of Parliament (MP) Damien O'Connor, in the Labour Party campaign launch video for the 2011 general election, described the trickle-down effect as "the rich pissing on the poor". A 2012 study by the Tax Justice Network indicates that wealth of the super-rich does not trickle down to improve the economy, but tends to be amassed and sheltered in tax havens with a negative effect on the tax base of the home economy

(Stewart 2012). Chang (2011) criticises trickle-down policies, citing examples of slowing job growth in the last few decades and rising income inequality in most rich nations. Dabla-Norris et al. (2015) suggest that if the income share of the top 20% rises, then GDP growth actually declines over the medium term, suggesting that the benefits do not trickle down. In contrast, an increase in the income share of the bottom 20% (the poor) is associated with higher GDP growth.

Tax reform as called for by the third commandment is a means whereby the rich get richer and the poor get poorer. It is conducive to the transfer of resources from the general public to the multinationals that prey on the people of those unfortunate countries that need IMF assistance. If in doubt, ask the Russians who went through a horrific experience in the early 1990s.

2.5   THE FOURTH COMMANDMENT: MARKET-DETERMINED INTEREST RATES

The declared objective here is to allow the market to determine interest rates and to keep real interest rates positive and moderate. This recommendation works against the practice of subsidising loans to the agricultural sector, which provides food. Again, this is not what is practised by the preaching countries, particularly since the advent of quantitative easing at the end of 2008. This form of monetary policy, which has killed the middle class and small savers, means that the market is manipulated to produce ultra-low nominal interest rates and negative real interest rates. In some countries, even nominal interest rates are negative. In Fig. 2.4 we observe the nominal short-term interest rates in the US, the UK, Japan and the Eurozone since October 2008. The US has reversed the low interest rate policy but in Europe interest rates are negative—customers pay banks for "looking after" their money, which is likely to be confiscated to "bail in" troubled banks. In early August 2018, Mark Carney, the Governor of the Bank of England, commented on the increase in British interest rates from 0.5% to 0.75% by saying that no one should worry about the effect of rising interest rates and that 5% is a thing of the past. Policy makers in the preaching countries do not realise that you can take the horse to water but you cannot make it drink. Investment is not interest elastic and if the outlook is pessimistic, economic activity will not bounce

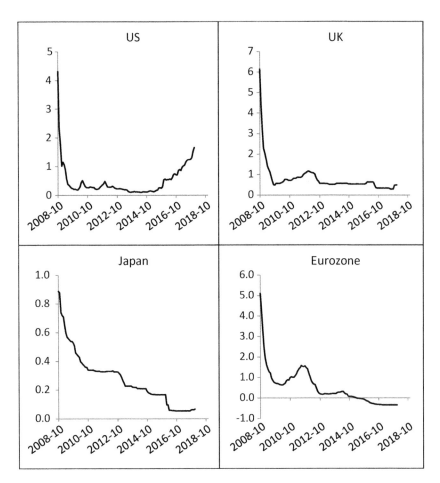

Fig. 2.4 Short-term interest rates

back, no matter how low interest rates are. Or it could be that policy makers know this but they keep interest rates low because that is what the
banksters want (and also because low interest rates reduce the cost of
financing unnecessary wars).

Market-determined interest rates tend to be volatile, creating interest rate
risk, which is difficult to manage in the absence of sophisticated financial
markets. In 1979, the Federal Reserve shifted from a policy of interest rate
targeting to a policy of money supply targeting, leading to a phenomenal rise

in (market-determined) interest rates and the recession of the early 1980s. Developing countries do not need the headache caused by interest rate volatility—rather they need subsidised agricultural loans.

In any case, the IMF invariably recommends higher interest rates in response to depreciating currencies. The underlying idea is that high interest rates make domestic currency-denominated deposits and other financial assets more attractive for foreign investors. High interest rates are also prescribed to control inflation, but they end up worsening the economic downturn. Stiglitz (2002) argues that while high interest rates are intended to control inflation, which may not be a problem to start with, they end up forcing the bankruptcy of countless otherwise productive companies that could not cope with a sudden rise in the cost of funding. Stiglitz also thinks that high interest rates may lead to overvalued currencies, which have to come down sooner or later, giving currency traders a one-way bet.

2.6   The Fifth Commandment: Maintaining "Competitive" Exchange Rates

It is not clear what a "competitive" exchange rate is, but one would imagine that it is the exchange rate that makes exports competitive in foreign markets. In this sense, a competitive exchange rate implies a weak domestic currency, which is a double-edged sword because a weak currency makes imports more expensive and brings in imported inflation. This is why countries strive to strike a balance by having their currencies neither too strong nor too weak. This, however, is not an easy task, since exchange rates are typically misaligned, falling above or below their equilibrium values. In Fig. 2.5 we observe the undervaluation or overvaluation of currencies against the US dollar as measured by the Big Mac index that was developed by *The Economist* in 1986. Misalignment is the rule rather than the exception.

What matters for competitiveness is the unobservable real exchange rate rather than the observable nominal exchange rate. The exchange rates of the preaching countries are typically misaligned, which makes the achievement of this objective almost impossible for the countries that are preached to. It seems, however, that this recommendation means keeping the domestic currency weak, which, when coupled with privatisation and the liberalisation of foreign direct investment, provides bargains for the multinationals taking part in the "sale of the century".

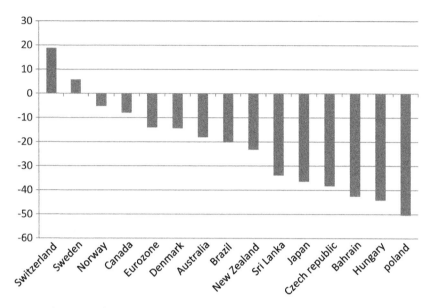

Fig. 2.5 Overvaluation (+) and undervaluation (−) against the US dollar (%)

2.7   THE SIXTH COMMANDMENT: TRADE LIBERALISATION

The sixth commandment of trade liberalisation refers particularly to the liberalisation of imports in the sense of eliminating quantitative restrictions while using "relatively low uniform tariffs" for the purpose of trade protection. This commandment rests on the proposition that free trade is always beneficial, which is not necessarily true. Free trade requires the following conditions: (i) the abolition of tariffs and other trade barriers (such as quotas on imports or subsidies for producers); (ii) trade in services without taxes or other trade barriers; (iii) the absence of "trade-distorting" policies (such as taxes, subsidies, regulations or laws) that give some firms, households or factors of production an advantage over others; (iv) unregulated access to markets; (v) unregulated access to market information; (vi) inability of domestic firms to distort markets through government-imposed monopoly or oligopoly power; and (vii) participation in trade agreements that encourage free trade. So, it is all about removing this and that piece of regulation because they "distort" trade—all, of course, for the benefit of big firms from the preaching countries.

Although free trade commands significant support from mainstream economists, who argue that it is beneficial, this view is not accepted universally. While developing countries are preached to on the benefits of free trade, the preaching countries adopted protectionism on a massive scale when they were at the same stage of economic development. Furthermore, free trade is a doctrine that is associated with British colonialism, seeking markets to extract cheap raw materials and markets for their products, the most notorious of which was the lucrative market for opium in China. What was at one time done by taking military action against countries that refuse unfettered access to their markets is now done by preaching free trade, by imposing sanctions or by using financial blackmail. This does not mean that military action is no longer used for the same purpose. Iraq has become a lucrative market for American military hardware following the invasion of 2003.

In a 2006 survey of American economists (83 responders), 87.5% agreed that the US should eliminate remaining tariffs and other barriers to trade and 90.1% disagreed with the proposition that the US should restrict employers from outsourcing work to foreign countries (Whaples 2006). In another survey of leading economists, none disagreed with the proposition that "freer trade improves productive efficiency and offers consumers better choices, and in the long run these gains are much larger than any effects on employment" (IGM Forum 2012). Mankiw (2006) expresses the view that "few propositions command as much consensus among professional economists as that open world trade increases economic growth and raises living standards".

Historically, the US practised protectionism on a grand scale until about 1945. In fact what is known as the "American System" of economics is a mercantilist system. The Republican Party led by Abraham Lincoln strongly opposed free trade and implemented a 44% tariff during the Civil War—in part to pay for railroad subsidies and for the war effort, and to protect favoured industries. William McKinley (1892) stated the stance of the Republican Party as follows:

> Under free trade the trader is the master and the producer the slave. Protection is but the law of nature, the law of self-preservation, of self-development, of securing the highest and best destiny of the race of man. [It is said] that protection is immoral. ... Why, if protection builds up and elevates 63,000,000 [the US population] of people, the influence of those 63,000,000 of people elevates the rest of the world. We cannot take a step

in the pathway of progress without benefitting mankind everywhere. Well, they say, 'Buy where you can buy the cheapest'. … Of course, that applies to labor as to everything else. Let me give you a maxim that is a thousand times better than that, and it is the protection maxim: 'Buy where you can pay the easiest'. And that spot of earth is where labor wins its highest rewards.

During the inter-war period, economic protectionism took hold in the US, most famously in the form of the Smoot-Hawley Tariff Act, which is believed to be responsible for the prolonging and worldwide propagation of the Great Depression. Chang (2002) notes that many of the now industrialised countries had significant barriers to trade throughout their history. America and Britain, the homes of free trade policy, employed protectionism to varying degrees at all times. In 1846 Britain abolished the Corn Laws, which restricted the import of grain in response to domestic pressures. In the mid-nineteenth century Britain reduced protectionism for manufactures when its technological advantage was at its height, but tariffs on manufactured products had returned to 23% by 1950. The US maintained weighted average tariffs on manufactured products of approximately 40–50% until the 1950s, augmented by the natural protectionism of high transportation costs in the nineteenth century. The most consistent practitioners of free trade have been Switzerland, the Netherlands and to a lesser degree Belgium. Chang describes the export-oriented industrialisation policies of the Asian Tigers as "far more sophisticated and fine-tuned than their historical equivalents".

Several arguments have been put forward against free trade and for protectionism. Free trade is opposed on the grounds that it destroys infant industries and undermines long-run economic development. It aggravates income inequality and environmental degradation, accentuates poverty in poor countries and forces undesirable cultural changes. Free trade is often opposed by domestic industries that would have their profits and market shares reduced by the lower prices of imported goods. Free trade agreements generally do not boost the economic freedom of the poor or the working class, and frequently make them poorer. If the foreign supplier is in the business of de facto exploitation of labour, domestic labour is unfairly forced to compete with the foreign exploited labour. Chris Hedges (2017) describes free trade deals by saying that they "legally empower global corporations to destroy small farmers and businesses and deindustrialise the country". Free trade is conducive to the subversion of workers' rights and provides the means to go around laws that protect individual liberty.

It has long been argued that free trade is a form of colonialism or imperialism, a position taken by various proponents of economic nationalism
and the school of mercantilism. In the nineteenth century, British calls for
free trade were criticised as a cover for the British Empire, notably in the
work of Henry Clay, architect of the American System, and by Friedrich
List. Clay (1832) said the following:

> Gentlemen deceive themselves. It is not free trade that they are recommend-
> ing to our acceptance. It is, in effect, the British colonial system that we are
> invited to adopt; and, if their policy prevails, it will lead, substantially, to the
> recolonization of these States, under the commercial dominion of Great
> Britain.

Likewise, List (1909) expressed the following view:

> Had the English left everything to itself—'Laissez faire, laissez aller', as the
> popular economical [sic] school recommends—the [German] merchants of
> the Steelyard would be still carrying on their trade in London, the Belgians
> would be still manufacturing cloth for the English, England would have still
> continued to be the sheep-farm of the Hansards, just as Portugal became
> the vineyard of England, and has remained so till our days, owing to the
> stratagem of a cunning diplomatist.

According to Chang (2002), however, it was Treasury Secretary
Alexander Hamilton, and not Friedrich List, who was the first to present a
systematic argument in defence of industrial protectionism. The last thing
to say in this respect is that if free trade is as good for everyone as it is
claimed by the Washington preachers, how did Donald Trump become
the president of the US in large part by promising war on free trade? And
it is a promise that he has kept.

We close this section on a sombre note on how the British Empire saw
free trade between Britain, Africa, the Caribbean and America. This is illustrated in Fig. 2.6, which depicts a pattern that lasted until the abolition of
slavery in 1833. Beginning in the last decade of the 1400s, free trade involved
the kidnapping of Africans, cramming them in ships and taking them to the
British colonies in the Caribbean and America. The lucrative "triangle of
trade" between the west coast of Africa, the Americas and Britain, involving
slaves, and the goods they were forced to produce, created the first lords of
modern capitalism such as John Hawkins, a slave trader, who made a massive
fortune in the 1560s. According to Manjapra (2018):

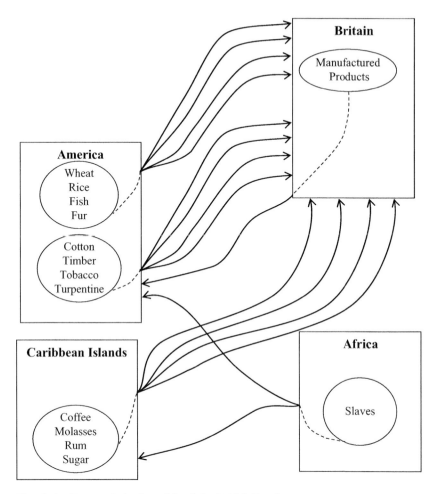

Fig. 2.6 Free trade in the spirit of the British Empire

From the 15th to the 19th centuries, more than 11 million shackled black captives were forcibly transported to the Americas, and unknown multitudes were lost at sea. Captives were often thrown overboard when they were too sick, or too strong-willed, or too numerous to feed. Those who survived the journey were dumped on the shores and sold to the highest bidder, then sold on again and again like financial assets.

According to Eric Williams, a historian of slavery who also became the first prime minister of independent Trinidad in 1962, slavery in the British Empire was only abolished after it had ceased to be economically useful (Manjapra 2018). We must add that in 1835 the British government borrowed the equivalent of £300 billion in today's money from the Rothschilds to finance "slave compensation" following the abolition of slavery. The compensation money went exclusively to the owners of slaves who had lost their "property". Britain practised the Washington Consensus before anyone had heard of Washington.

2.8   THE SEVENTH COMMANDMENT: LIBERALISATION OF INWARD FDI

The rationale for the seventh commandment is that foreign direct investment (FDI) confers benefits on the host country. However, this is far from being a foregone conclusion as the benefits of FDI to the host country constitute a controversial and debatable topic. Let us consider in turn each of the perceived benefits of FDI by assuming that the host country has a developing economy whereas the source country is the home country of the multinational corporations (MNCs) indulging in FDI in the host country.

The first perceived benefit is that FDI flows continue to expand even when world trade slows down or when portfolio investment dries up. FDI flows are less volatile than portfolio investment flows because FDI represents a long-term commitment to the underlying project. This argument is not convincing because the distinction between the flows of portfolio investment and FDI may be blurred. Both may involve the purchase of shares in the host country, the only difference being that an investment in shares is considered FDI if the investor has a big stake that enables the exertion of some control. The IMF's *Balance of Payments Manual* defines FDI as "an investment that is made to acquire a lasting interest in an enterprise operating in an economy other than that of the investor, the investor's purpose being to have an effective voice in the management of the enterprise". The common feature of various definitions of FDI lies in words like "control" and "controlling interest", which represent the characteristic that distinguishes FDI from portfolio investment, since a portfolio investor does not seek control or lasting interest. While there is no agreement on what constitutes a controlling interest, a minimum of 10%

shareholding is commonly regarded as allowing the foreign firm to exert a significant influence, either potentially or actually exercised, over the key policies of the underlying project. Furthermore, measuring FDI is not an easy task, which explains why gaps are observed in the FDI statistics. This makes it difficult to verify the assertion that FDI is stable and less volatile. After all, selling a 10% stake in a company in the host country (FDI) is as easy or difficult as selling a 5% stake in the same company (portfolio investment). Even with other forms of FDI that do not involve shareholding, divestment can happen quickly and so does the repatriation of profit.

The second alleged benefit is that FDI involves the transfer of financial capital, technology and other skills desperately needed by developing countries. Technology diffusion and the transfer of capital boost growth in host countries, whereas the provision of training enhances the skills of local workers. However, FDI is often blamed for creating balance of payments problems for the host country because of profit repatriation. FDI does not play an important role in technology diffusion because of (i) the inappropriateness of the technology provided as it tends to be too capital-intensive; (ii) the availability of cheaper sources of technology; and (iii) research and development (R&D) activities that are concentrated in the MNCs' home countries. The cost of training labour is not high enough to make a significant contribution to the improvement of the skills of local workers. The practices of MNCs may be irrelevant to the host country, in which case training is not useful and may even be harmful. Moreover, it is often the case that MNCs reserve key managerial and technical positions for expatriates. FDI does not perform the function of providing capital for three reasons: (i) it is a relatively expensive source of financial capital; (ii) actual capital flows provided by MNCs will not be large if they choose to obtain funds from the local capital market; and (iii) the capital contribution of MNCs may take non-financial form (e.g., goodwill). By raising capital locally, MNCs crowd out domestic investment, which is perhaps more suitable than foreign investment.

The third benefit is that FDI has a positive effect on income and social welfare in the host country in the absence of distortions caused by protection, monopoly and externalities. If anything, FDI itself creates monopolies. Blaming the failure of the positive effects to materialise on protection is convenient for MNCs to do as they please. MNCs exist and operate primarily because of market imperfections, which preclude the conditions under which FDI supposedly boosts welfare. And even if FDI boosts output, it results in some undesirable distributional changes between labour and capital. Furthermore, FDI creates enclaves and foreign elite in the host country and introduces adverse cultural changes. MNCs indulge in the production of luxury goods rather than the basic consumer goods needed in developing countries. MNCs worsen income distribution in host countries and worldwide by paying foreign workers low wages, charging ordinary consumers high (sometimes extortionist) prices and paying "celebrities" obscene amounts of money for sponsoring their products. They also abuse transfer pricing, depriving host countries of tax revenue.

The fourth perceived benefit of FDI is that it boosts employment in the host country by setting up new production facilities, by stimulating employment in distribution, and by acquiring and restructuring ailing firms. It is also likely to have a positive effect on productivity if (i) it is export-promoting and (ii) the underlying conditions allow the installation of plants designed to realise economies of scale. However, the domination of a developing country by an MNC may be detrimental to growth through a lower rate of capital accumulation, greater incidence of undesirable practices and adverse effect on competition. FDI can reduce employment through divestment and closure of production facilities. The empirical evidence shows that the overall employment effects of the activities of MNCs on the host country are small. FDI leads to an increase in wage inequality in the host country and to a worsening of market concentration, as well as the possibility of monopolistic or oligopolistic practices.

FDI has other adverse consequences. In some cases it symbolises new colonialism and it results in the loss of sovereignty and in compromising national security. MNCs are known to interfere with the politics of the host country—for example, the Chilean coup of 1973 (the Chilean 9/11) was instigated by AT&T. MNCs are often in a position to obtain incentives (from the host country) in excess of their needs and typically in excess of the benefits they bring to the host country. They are very powerful negotiators, likely to strike favourable terms in bilateral negotiations with the government of a poor country. They form alliances with corrupt elites in developing countries.

FDI is also a source of pollution and corruption. The pollution haven hypothesis, or pollution haven effect, is the proposition that polluting industries tend to relocate to jurisdictions with less stringent environmental regulations. For example, spent batteries that Americans turn in to be recycled are increasingly being sent to Mexico, where the lead inside them is extracted by crude methods that are illegal in the US. FDI can be motivated by the difference between more stringent domestic environmental regulation and comparatively lax regulation in the FDI destination country. The "helping-hand" theory, which describes the relation between FDI and corruption in the host country, states that rather than being an obstacle for business, corruption provides the "lubrication" needed to deal with rigid economic regulation and red-tape. By bribing the host government, MNCs could get around regulations or red-tape and potentially obtain benefits in terms of lucrative contracts and privileged access to markets and subsidies, which would act as an extra incentive for them to engage in FDI (hence the effect is positive). Tanzi (1998) points out that decisions to authorise major FDI projects often provide MNCs with monopoly power in the host country, which would be extremely profitable, providing incentives for MNCs to bribe host government officials. As a result, a corrupt host government would be preferred by an MNC over an honest one.

Kaufmann (1997) refers to the "helping-hand" theory as a "revisionist view", citing Leff (1964) as expressing the view that "corruption may introduce an element of competition into what is otherwise a comfortably monopolistic industry" and that "payment of the highest bribes [becomes] one of the principal criteria for allocation". He also cites Liu (1985) as arguing that "bribing strategies ... minimize the average value of the time costs of the queue" and that the official "could choose to speed up the service when bribery is allowed". A related argument is that bribery allows supply and demand to operate, in the sense that under competitive bidding for a government procurement contract, the highest briber will win while the lowest-cost firm will be able to afford the highest bribe. Kaufmann suggests that corruption is negatively associated with developmental objectives everywhere and that opportunistic bureaucrats and politicians, who try to maximise their take without regard for the impact of such perdition on the "size of the overall pie", may account for the particularly adverse impact of corruption.

It seems therefore that FDI is a double-edged sword—far from being always benign. The seventh commandment is designed for the benefit of MNCs by providing unlimited access to cheap labour and other resources and open markets. The cost to the host country could be enormous. If corruption can be justified in the name of efficiency, then any adverse consequence of FDI for the host country can be justified, including the killing of hundreds of thousands in the Chilean 9/11 or the killing of thousands in Bhopal, India, by a foreign direct investor who literally got away with murder.

2.9   THE EIGHTH COMMANDMENT: PRIVATISATION
OF STATE ENTERPRISES

Privatisation is the process of transferring the ownership of public enterprises and assets to the private sector. On the surface, this sounds good as the assets will be owned by ordinary people and public enterprises become more efficient when they are run by entrepreneurs rather than government bureaucrats. This, however, is not entirely true because privatisation is essentially a means of transferring the ownership of public assets to oligarchs and multinationals in a process that involves widespread corruption, leading to worsening income and wealth inequality. Once public assets are transferred to private hands, a process of "restructuring" follows in the name of efficiency whereby thousands of people lose their jobs while the CEO and his or her inner circle get their salaries and bonuses increased by a factor of 100. This proposition is not a product of economic analysis but rather of simple observation. Look no further than Russia in the early 1990s when Boris Yeltsin, the darling of the "west", squandered public assets while under the effect of massive doses of vodka in a process marred by corruption and favouritism. Yeltsin's privatisation programme created the Russian oligarchy and mafia while ordinary people could not afford to bury their dead. The oligarchs ended up smuggling their money, primarily to London. It is therefore natural for the "west" to hate Vladimir Putin for renationalising Russia's largest and most successful company, the Yukos oil company, as well as a number of companies in the strategic sectors of the economy.

The arguments put forward to advocate privatisation are based on improvement in efficiency, output and profitability, particularly if the industry is competitive. These improvements are supposed to arise out of enhanced incentives to innovate and reduce costs, which tend to have a positive impact on economic growth. Even though some studies reveal that these benefits are associated with costs, the costs (adverse consequences) can be dealt with by appropriate government support through redistribution and retraining (Nellis and Kikeri 2002; Megginson and Netter 2001; Birdsall and Nellis 2003). Yet, some studies suggest that privatisation could have very modest effects on efficiency and a quite regressive distributive impact. In the first attempt at a social welfare analysis of the British privatisation programme under the Conservative governments of Margaret Thatcher and John Major during the 1980s and 1990s, Massimo (2004) points to the absence of any productivity shock resulting strictly from ownership change.

The empirical evidence presented in favour of privatisation does not stand up to the observation that privatisation typically involves large-scale corruption, as those with political connections unfairly gain large wealth. The pundits respond to this observation by suggesting that in addition to improved operating efficiency, daily petty corruption is, or would be, larger without privatisation, and that corruption is more prevalent in non-privatised sectors. Furthermore, some evidence suggests that extra-legal and unofficial activities are more prevalent in countries that did not go far enough in the privatisation game (Nellis and Kikeri 2002; Martimort and Straub 2006). On the other hand, a 2009 study published in *The Lancet* medical journal claimed to have found that as many as a million working men died as a result of the economic shocks associated with mass privatisation in the former Soviet Union and Eastern Europe during the 1990s (Medical Express 2009). The *Lancet* study found that the so-called shock therapy led to a 56% increase in unemployment, with the loss of extensive health and social care. Through privatisation workers experienced the "double whammy" of losing not only their livelihood but also the means of surviving the crisis.

Arguments for privatisation (against public ownership) are typically based on the imaginary benefits of a free market. The first argument against public ownership is that state-run industries tend to be bureaucratic, motivated to improve performance only when the underlying issue becomes politically sensitive. Who cares about bureaucracy and motivation if the public enterprise provides cheap goods and services for everyone? A bureaucratic state-run hospital providing free medical care for all citizens is better than an "unbureaucratic" private hospital that prices everyone out apart from the top 1% (e.g., by charging $5000 a night for the bed only, much more expensive than any seven-start hotel). A related argument is that of efficiency, in the sense that private firms have a greater incentive to produce goods and services more efficiently to boost profits. The so-called efficiency may result from redundancies and cutting corners, which cannot be good for the society as a whole. A strange argument is that of specialisation—that is, a private firm can specialise, but a public firm cannot. Another argument is based on corruption, that publicly owned companies are prone to corruption in the sense that decisions are made for the personal gain of the decision maker. We will talk about corruption in Chap. 3 and show how corrupt the privately owned "western" financial institutions are. This of course does not mean that non-financial institutions are not corrupt.

Then there is an argument based on accountability, as the managers of privately owned companies are accountable to shareholders whereas the managers of publicly owned companies are required to be more accountable to the broader community. Tell that to the shareholders of Merrill Lynch and Enron who lost everything as the managers enriched themselves (and there is more where that came from). The managers, supposedly acting for the benefit of shareholders, have one objective function: maximisation of their own wealth before receiving a golden parachute. What is wrong with being accountable to the broader community? Is it not the case that when a firm is accountable to the community, it considers marginal social costs rather than marginal private costs? Then of course there are civil-liberty concerns in the sense that a firm controlled by the state may have access to information that can be used against dissidents or any individuals who disagree with their policies. This is a truly strange argument in an age when civil liberties have all but gone in the name of national security. Governments in the "free world" have been confiscating civil liberties and spy on people with the help of private sector firms.

One argument for privatisation is that state-owned companies are run in such a way as to achieve political goals whereas private sector companies are run to achieve economic goals. We assume that economic goals imply one objective only, which is profit maximisation by any means, including the destruction of the environment. Another argument is that private firms are in a better position to raise capital in financial markets. We suppose that this argument is not valid for a developing country that has rudimentary financial markets and whose companies cannot borrow in overseas markets because of country risk considerations.

Then listen to this argument: governments have the tendency to bail out poorly run businesses, often due to the sensitivity of job losses when it may be better to let the business go. Well, the concept of "too big to fail" was invented in the "west", the land of free enterprise, where private sector companies (particularly banks) are bailed out with taxpayers' money, not because of the fear of job losses, but so that the CEO and his or her inner circle (senior management) get their bonuses. It is ironic that the first too-big-to-fail rescue of a bank was made in 1984 on the watch of Ronald Reagan, a champion of free markets and privately owned firms. Nowadays, governments in the "free world" are working on bail-in legislation to save the CEOs of failed banks by confiscating customer deposits. A related argument is that poorly managed state companies are insulated from the same discipline as private companies, which could go bankrupt, have their management removed or be taken over by competitors. The fact of the matter is that private sector companies are not that disciplined. CEOs tend to take excessive risks to maximise short-run gains, and when they are removed they receive massive golden parachutes and live happily ever after. Those CEOs get their bonuses and parachutes even if their companies are making losses or stock prices are retreating (see, e.g., Moosa 2016).

Pro-privatisation thinkers believe that the existence of natural monopolies does not mean that these sectors must be state owned because governments can use anti-trust legislation to deal with anti-competitive behaviour. In reality, market concentration is the status quo, and there is no evidence to suggest that the use of anti-trust legislation is effective in dealing with anti-competitive behaviour, particularly because of political capture. Then there is the argument that ownership of and profits from successful (private) enterprises tend to be dispersed and diversified. However, a look at the distribution of share ownership tells us otherwise, as the distribution is as skewed as the distribution of wealth. The claim that privatisation is conducive to job creation is counterfactual, as every episode of privatisation has been accompanied by massive job losses.

The proponents of privatisation claim that nationalised industries are prone to interference from politicians for political or populist reasons—for example, making an industry buy supplies from local producers (when that may be more expensive than buying from abroad), forcing an industry to freeze its prices to satisfy the electorate or control inflation, increasing its staffing to reduce unemployment or moving its operations to marginal constituencies. Are these not exactly the same policies that got Donald Trump elected? This is perhaps what people want. A government that acts in response to the wishes of the general population is better than a government that acts only in the interest of big business because government decision makers hope to be rewarded with high-pay jobs after leaving government. And it is definitely better than a government that launches wars on defenceless countries for the benefit of (private sector) war profiteers.

The opponents of certain privatisations believe that some public goods and services should remain primarily in the hands of government in order to ensure that everyone in society has access to them (such as law enforcement, basic healthcare and basic education). There is a positive externality when the government provides public goods and services such as disease control. In theory at least, a democratically elected government is accountable to the people through a legislature and it is motivated to safeguard the assets of the nation. Most importantly, the profit motive may be sub-ordinated to social objectives as the enterprise considers social rather than private costs.

We have seen what has happened as a result of the privatisation of higher education, healthcare and utilities. Higher education has been in perpetual decline in the "western" world as universities advertise their services and students become customers. The quality of graduates is so bad because private universities are sausage machines, interested only in profit maximisation and customer satisfaction. The right to higher education has been supplanted by the "right" to have access to a student loan that cripples the life of a new graduate as higher education has become a good that is bought and sold and whose price is determined in a free market by the forces of supply and demand. Chris Hedges (2017) describes the state of higher education by saying that "the educational system is being privatized and turned into a species of rogue vocational training". The privatisation of healthcare means that only the rich get looked after. If you need a life-saving operation but you cannot pay for it, then you are left to die in the name of efficiency or because the market says so. The privatisation of utilities has led to the death of many people who cannot afford to pay their gas bills. Typically, the owners of a privatised utility company abandon social obligation to those who are less able to pay, or to regions where this service is unprofitable.

Even if we talk about the provision of goods and services, there is no reason why public enterprises could not do as good a job as private enterprises. In what way has the privatisation of British Rail and British Airways led to a better performance? Is not the British Broadcasting Corporation (BBC), which is publicly owned, a source of pride for Britain? In Australia, the publicly owned Australian Broadcasting Corporation (ABC) and Special Broadcasting Service (SBS) are far superior to the privately owned Channel 7, Channel 9 and Channel 10, which present advertisements interrupted by poor-quality programmes. It is easier for governments to exert pressure on state-owned firms to help implement policy and to make them compliant with the provisions of environmental regulation. Private firms serve the needs of those who are most willing (and able) to pay, as opposed to the needs of the majority—hence private firms are anti-democratic. For necessary goods, demand is highly (if not perfectly) inelastic, in which case the majority of people will be exploited or excluded if those goods are provided by the private sector.

Privatisation leads to poverty and aggravates the distribution of income and wealth as job losses mount. It leads to lower wages (apart from the salaries of top management), hence aggravating poverty. It leads to deteriorating working conditions, again in the name of efficiency. And it leads to inferior quality products as companies cut corners in the name of efficiency (look no further than private higher education these days). Privatisation produces a few winners (the oligarchs, the politically connected and multinationals) and far too many losers (the majority of the population).

We should not forget that the profitable business of private prisons, which has led to the mass incarceration of people who do not even get a trial through the short cut of a "plea bargain". The "land of the free" houses no less than 25% of the world prison population because of the "efficiency" of private prisons. Chris Hedges (2017) mentions private prisons in his magnificent 2017 speech, saying the following:

> Our system of mass incarceration is not broken—it works exactly the way it is designed to work. The bodies of poor people of color do not generate money for corporations on the streets of our deindustrialised cities but they generate 40 or 50 thousand dollars a year if we lock them in cages and that is why they are there. … One million prisoners now work for corporations inside prisons as modern day slaves, paid pennies on the dollar without any rights or protection. They are the corporate state's ideal workers.

The business of private armies, such as Blackwater or whatever it is called these days, has become profitable and efficient but only at the expense of the hundreds of thousands of dead, injured or displaced by wars initiated against countries that cannot fight back. The private military industry has become so profitable because the US is dropping one bomb every 12 minutes. George Bush Jr. dropped 70,000 bombs in five countries; the Nobel Peace Prize winner Barack Obama dropped 100,000 bombs in seven countries; Donald Trump dropped 44,000 bombs in his first year alone—one bomb every 12 minutes. Let us also not forget that the underground economy is a private sector activity. This sector has become efficient in drug and people trafficking as well as murder, kidnapping and torture.

More bizarre than private prisons is private mining. When a country is blessed with natural resources, one would tend to think that those resources should be extracted by a public enterprise to generate revenue that can be used to finance public expenditure, particularly health, education and welfare. Nothing is inefficient about this kind of arrangement. What we see, however, is that the right to extract resources is granted somehow to an individual or a company that digs the stuff and sells it for private profit, paying pennies in royalties. In one country in the southern hemisphere, this kind of arrangement produced a person who is one of the richest people on the planet, while the population is burdened with heavy taxes and the rate of homelessness is on the increase. At one time, the sitting prime minister put forward a proposal to introduce a mining tax, only to find himself replaced in a de facto coup by his deputy who promptly abandoned the plan. If that coup had happened in an African rather than a "western" country, it would have been condemned as undemocratic, but it is fine in a "western" democracy. If anything, mining companies should be nationalised for the benefit of the people at large.

Private enterprise leads to imperialism and regime change. By enticing politicians and generals with lucrative jobs after leaving public service, the private sector is in a position to utilise the military and intelligence services for the purpose of profit maximisation through invasion and regime change. Japanese imperialism arose out of the private sector's insatiable appetite for raw materials and markets. The opium war was launched by Britain against China to protect the private enterprise selling opium to the Chinese. A private telecommunication company is responsible for the Chilean 9/11 in which tens of thousands of people perished. It was King Leopold's private enterprise that led to the wiping out of half the population of what used to be called the Belgian Congo. Numerous bloody coups have been orchestrated by oil companies to put in place friendly regimes. Let us not forget that the Nazis indulged in privatisation in Germany during the period 1933–1937, when the government sold off public ownership in several state-owned firms belonging to a wide range of sectors, including steel, mining, banking, public utilities, shipyards, shipping lines and railways. The delivery of some public services produced by public enterprises prior to the 1930s was transferred to the private sector, mainly to several organisations within the Nazi Party.

2.10   THE NINTH COMMANDMENT: DEREGULATION

Deregulation is the process of removing or reducing state regulations, typically in the economic sphere. At one time regulation was seen as necessary to contain the effect of externalities such as corporate abuse, unsafe child labour, monopoly and pollution. Around the late 1970s, free-market economics and neoliberalism became fashionable and widely accepted by politicians on both sides of the Atlantic. As a result, regulation was seen as burdensome for economic growth, while government intervention in economic activity was thought to produce adverse unintended consequences, including "inefficiency". There was also the risk that regulatory agencies would be controlled by the regulated industry to its benefit, and thereby hurt consumers and the wider economy. It was also believed that a trend towards deregulation would boost economic welfare.

The opponents of regulation, typically free marketeers, put forward several explanations for deregulation. First, deregulation boosts competitiveness, productivity and efficiency, consequently producing lower prices for the benefit of consumers. Second, it is possible to remove the cause of market failure by technological or demand factors (e.g., a monopolistic market becomes a competitive market). Third, more efficient alternatives to regulation are available for solving the problem of market failure. Fourth, shifts can occur in the relative political power of pressure groups—for example, as a result of more efficient combatting of the free-rider problem. Fifth, deregulation may arise when politically effective groups believe that they can promote their economic interests more effectively in an unregulated market—for example, by self-regulation. Sixth, deregulation can be the result of declining profits, so that the political yield of regulation declines. Last, but not least, deregulation can be accounted for by rising deadweight costs over time because substitutes for regulated products are developed and because costly methods of evading and avoiding particular regulations are discovered. None of these arguments is stronger than the argument that deregulation played a major role in the advent of the global financial crisis and various mishaps (including pollution, fraud and criminal offences) all around the world. We were told that the financial system could regulate itself but that turned not to be the case, as self-regulation boils down to allowing the inmates to run the asylum.

Cali et al. (2008) suggest that service liberalisation should be accompanied by regulation as the provision of services is typically characterised by elements of natural monopoly and informational asymmetries. Hence regulation is required to ensure that service markets work properly to accomplish the following specific objectives: (i) to create a level playing field and ensure competition between market players (e.g., in ensuring a sufficient number of telecommunication providers); (ii) to maintain the quality of services (e.g., by specifying qualification requirements for service providers); (iii) to protect consumers from fraud and malpractices; (iv) to ensure sufficient provision of information about the features of competing services; (v) to prevent environmental degradation; (vi) to guarantee wide access to services (such as electricity and healthcare); and (vii) to maintain financial stability and protect consumer savings from excessive risk taking by financial institutions.

On the deregulation of the electricity sector, Beder (2003) argues that while electricity deregulation was supposed to bring lower electricity prices and greater choice of suppliers, it has brought wildly volatile wholesale prices and undermined the reliability of supply. She further writes the following:

> The rising electricity prices and blackouts in California and the northeastern states of the US are consequences of the changes engineered by vested interests; changes that were accomplished through a massive PR campaign to deceive politicians and opinion leaders about their benefits. Despite efforts to manufacture an appearance of grassroots support, deregulation was primarily driven by large industrial users, who thought they could save money, and energy companies, who thought they could make money out of it.

In his defence of deregulation, Thierer (1998) argues that "the first step toward creating a free market in electricity is to repeal the federal statutes and regulations that hinder electricity competition and consumer choice". He suggests "five simple steps" to deregulate the electricity market: (i) eliminating, reforming or phasing out federal electricity laws and programmes; (ii) mandating the implementation of pro-competition, open-access policies at the state level by a specific date; (iii) restricting utility bailouts that could strangle competition at the outset and unconstitutionally burden interstate commerce; (iv) privatising federal public power entities immediately to level the playing field; and (v) refraining from imposing any new environmental mandates. That worked definitely for the benefit of companies like Enron, which Beder (2003) deals with extensively.

Financial regulation can be justified in terms of the objective of maintaining financial stability. If corruption is a cause of financial crises, then corruption provides solid justification for financial regulation. Corruption is perceived to be a cause of the global financial crisis. One of the conclusions of the Financial Crisis Inquiry Commission is that "there was a systemic breakdown in accountability and ethics" (FCIC 2011). This is what the Commission had to say:

We witnessed an erosion of standards of responsibility and ethics that exacerbated the financial crisis. This was not universal, but these breaches stretched from the ground level to the corporate suites. They resulted not only in significant financial consequences but also in damage to the trust of investors, businesses, and the public in the financial system.

The subprime crisis of 2007 is also perceived to have been caused by corruption. Dowd (2009) views the subprime crisis of 2007 as a scandal and a "giant Ponzi scheme", which was enabled by the "financial innovation" of securitisation. The same can be said of the savings and loan (S&L) crisis. In his book *The Best Way to Rob a Bank is to Own One*, William Black describes in detail the complex network of collusion between bankers, regulators and legislators that brought about the S&L crisis of the 1980s (Black 2005). Black obtained an insider's knowledge of details that are not generally known because he was a lawyer working for the Federal Home Loan Bank Board during the presidency of the big deregulator, Ronald Reagan. Fraud was enabled by accounting conventions whose fraud-friendly rules helped hide the true extent of the collapse for a long period. The episode involved a Ponzi scheme that was in operation as bad banks were allowed to buy other banks, using phantom capital, which affected the S&L industry. Ironically, it was a Reagan appointee and a deregulation advocate, Edwin Gray, who ultimately revealed and stopped the fraud. Gray was an enthusiastic deregulator until he saw the consequences in the form of Ponzi schemes, real estate bubbles and derelict construction projects.

What would happen in a world without regulation? Well, the following have happened in a world with regulation (Moosa and Ramiah 2014): (i) widespread production and distribution of fake medicines, marketed as genuine; (ii) the marketing of beef infected with the mad-cow disease virus; (iii) the marketing of food products containing horse meat but labelled "beef"; (iv) trade in fake aircraft parts marketed as genuine ones; (v) the selling in some poor countries of bread made of flour mixed with sawdust; (vi) faulty building materials or less-than-adequate construction standards that eventually lead to the collapse of a building (or a bridge); (vii) compromising safety standards in dealing with hazardous chemicals (recall the Bhopal disaster in 1984); (viii) compromising the safety standards of the disposal of toxic waste, particularly by multinationals operating in developing countries; (ix) unscrupulous financiers, such as Bernie Madoff, running Ponzi schemes and ripping off clients; and (x) companies reporting false financial statements to cover losses or scandals (Enron is one notorious example).

The true motivation for deregulation is that regulation hurts the bottom line of big business. Is this a good enough reason for allowing big business to destroy the environment and defraud people? Deregulation makes life much easier for big corporate entities as they can do what they want to maximise profit. No wonder then that a business tycoon like Donald Trump managed to destroy the US Environmental Protection Agency by appointing a deregulator and a global warming denier to head the Agency.

2.11   The Tenth Commandment: Legal Security for Property Rights

The enforcement of property rights is important. In fact it is believed that the industrial revolution took place in Britain not because of technology but because of the presence of a working system of patents and property rights. At one time, China was technologically advanced and so was the Muslim world, but no industrial revolution occurred there because of the lack of property rights. Both Adam Smith and Karl Marx recognised the importance of property rights in the process of economic development, and modern mainstream economics agrees with such recognition. Property rights are also believed to reduce transaction costs by providing an efficient resolution for conflicts over scarce resources.

A widely accepted explanation for the positive effect of property rights is that a well-enforced system provides incentives for individuals to participate in and contribute to investment, innovation and trade. Historically, the lack of protection for property rights provided little incentive for landowners and merchants to invest in land, physical or human capital, or technology. After the Civil War of 1642 and the Glorious Revolution of 1688, shifts of political power away from the Stuart monarchs led to strengthening of property rights of both land and capital owners. Consequently, rapid economic development took place, setting the stage for the industrial revolution.

In the Washington Consensus, this commandment is intended mainly to serve the privileges of foreign investors, particularly as they take hold of public assets through privatisation. The objective is to perpetuate foreign ownership even though it might have been made possible by a corrupt government like the government of Boris Yeltsin. Putin is criticised for trying to reverse some of the damage inflicted on Russia by Yeltsin—in the process Putin did the right thing by violating property rights.

2.12   CONCLUDING REMARKS

The Washington Consensus refers to a set of broadly free-market economic ideas, supported by international organisations, such as the IMF, the World Bank and the governments of "western" countries. It is associated with neoliberalism, involving policies encouraging free trade, privatisation, deregulation, a reduced size of government and "flexible" labour markets. Neoliberalism is associated with the policies of austerity and attempts to reduce budget deficits, typically by cutting government spending on social programmes. These neoliberal ideas were used in Chile in the late 1970s under the military dictatorship of General Pinochet, in Russia post-communism and in Greece during the Greek debt crisis. In the most recent episode of Greece, European Union (EU) officials demanded the adoption of various "reforms" in return for a bailout. The three episodes had disastrous effects on the general population.

Neoliberalism is responsible for the creation of the corporate state. Chris Hedges (2017) refers to what he calls the "corporate coup", saying the following:

> Corporations are legally empowered to exploit and loot. It is impossible to vote against Goldman Sachs and Exxon Mobile. The pharmaceutical and insurance industries are legally empowered to hold sick children hostage while their parents frantically bankrupt themselves trying to save their sons or daughters. Banks are legally empowered to burden people with student loans that cannot be forgiven by declaring bankruptcy. The animal agricultural industry is legally empowered to charge those who attempt to publicise the conditions in the vast factory farms where diseased animals are warehoused for slaughter, with a criminal offence. Corporations are legally empowered to carry out tax boycotts.

Essentially the adoption of these neoliberal ideas is nothing less than a complete rewriting of the implicit social contracts that have existed since the end of World War II, with the rise of the welfare state. In the rewritten social contracts, renewed legitimacy was bestowed on the laissez-faire policies once totally discredited following the Great Depression. As a result, privatisation, liberalisation and deregulation have become more important for progress than childcare, education, health, employment, disability and old age. The major beneficiaries of neoliberalism are MNCs and wealthy investors. Unfortunately, the principles of neoliberalism are widely held with near-religious fervour by most major political parties in the US and the UK and they are gaining acceptance by those holding power elsewhere. In cases where they are not accepted, they are imposed by financial, and sometimes military, force.

REFERENCES

Beder, S. (2003). The Electricity Deregulation Con Game. *PR Watch*, Center for Media and Democracy, *10*(3).

Birdsall, N., & Nellis, J. (2003). Winners and Losers: Assessing the Distributional Impact of Privatisation. *World Development, 31*, 1617–1633.

Black, W. K. (2005). *The Best Way to Rob a Bank is to Own One: How Corporate Executives and Politicians Looted the S&L Industry*. Austin: University of Texas Press.

Cali, M., Ellis, K., & te Velde, D. W. (2008). The Contribution of Services to Development: The Role of Regulation and Trade Liberalisation. Overseas Development Institute, Project Briefing No. 17.

Chang, H. J. (2002). *Kicking Away the Ladder: Development Strategy in Historical Perspective*. London: Anthem Press.

Chang, H. J. (2011). *23 Things They Don't Tell You About Capitalism*. New York: Bloomsbury Press.

Clay, H. (1832). *In Defense of the American System, Against the British Colonial System*. Washington, DC: Gales and Seaton.

Dabla-Norris, E., Kochhar, K., Suphaphiphat, N., Ricka, F., & Tsounta, E. (2015, June). Causes and Consequences of Income Inequality: A Global Perspective. *IMF Staff Discussion Note*.

Dowd, K. (2009). Moral Hazard and the Financial Crisis. *Cato Journal, 29*, 141–166.

FCIC. (2011). *The Financial Crisis Inquiry Report*. Washington, DC: US Government Printing Office.

Giangreco, D. M., & Moore, K. (1999). *Dear Harry: Truman's Mailroom, 1945–1953*. Mechanicsburg: Stackpole Books.

Greenspan, A. (2010, June 18). The US Debt and the Greece Analogy. *Wall Street Journal*.

Greider, W. (1981, December). The Education of David Stockman. *The Atlantic*.

Greider, W. (1982). *The Education of David Stockman and other Americans*. New York: Penguin.

Hedges, C. (2017). Speech. https://www.youtube.com/watch?v=Ycuw9Cvh6W4

IGM Forum. (2012, March 13). Free Trade. http://www.igmchicago.org/surveys/free-trade

Kaufmann, D. (1997). Corruption: The Facts. *Foreign Policy, 107*, 104–131.

Kotlikoff, L. J. (2006, July/August). Is the United States Bankrupt? *Federal Reserve Bank of St. Louis Review*, 235–249.

Leff, N. H. (1964). Economic Development through Bureaucratic Corruption. *American Behavioral Scientist, 8*, 8–14.

List, F. (1909). *The National System of Political Economy*. London: Longman, Green and Company.

Liu, F. T. (1985). An Equilibrium Queuing Model of Bribery. *Journal of Political Economy, 93*, 760–781.

Manjapra, K. (2018, March 29). When Will Britain Face Up to Its Crimes Against Humanity? *The Guardian*.

Mankiw, G. (2006). Outsourcing Redux. http://gregmankiw.blogspot.com/2006/05/outsourcing-redux.html

Martimort, D., & Straub, S. (2006). Privatisation and Corruption. Working Paper. http://idei.fr/sites/default/files/medias/doc/conf/veol/straub_martimort.pdf

Massimo, F. (2004). *The Great Divestiture: Evaluating the Welfare Impact of the British Privatizations, 1979–1997*. Cambridge, MA: MIT Press.

McKinley, W. (1892). Speech on October 4, 1892 in Boston. William McKinley Papers, Library of Congress, Washington, DC.

Medical Express. (2009). Death Surge Linked with Mass Privatisation. https://medicalxpress.com/news/2009-01-death-surge-linked-mass-privatisation.html

Megginson, W. L., & Netter, M. (2001). From State to Market: A Survey of Empirical Studies on Privatisation. *Journal of Economic Literature, 34*, 321–389.

Moosa, I. A. (2016). *Contemporary Issues in the Post-Crisis Regulatory Landscape*. Singapore: World Scientific.

Moosa, I. A., & Ramiah, V. (2014). *The Costs and Benefits of Environmental Regulation*. Cheltenham: Edward Elgar.

Nellis, J., & Kikeri, S. (2002, April). Privatisation in Competitive Sectors: The Record to Date. World Bank Policy Research Working Papers, No. 2860.

Peter Peterson Foundation. (2010). State of the Union Finances: A Citizen's Guide. http://www.google.com.au/search?q=%22State+of+the+Union+Finances%3A+A+Citizen%E2%80%99s+Guide%22&ie=utf-8&oe=utf-8&aq=t&rls=org.mozilla:en-US:official&client=firefox-a

Rodrik, D. (2006). Goodbye Washington Consensus, Hello Washington Confusion? A Review of the World Bank's Economic Growth in the 1990s: Learning from a Decade of Reform. *Journal of Economic Literature, 44*, 973–987.

Samuelson, R. J. (2009, May 18). Barack Obama's Risky Deficit Spending. *Real Clear Markets*. http://www.realclearmarkets.com/articles/2009/05/barack_obamas_risky_deficit_sp.html

Sims, A., & Boyle, D. (2009). *The New Economics: A Bigger Picture*. London: Earthscan.

Stewart, H. (2012, July 22). Wealth Doesn't Trickle Down – It just Floods Offshore. *The Guardian.*

Stiglitz, J. E. (2002). *Globalization and its Discontents.* New York: Norton.

Tanzi, V. (1998). Corruption Around the World: Causes, Consequences, Scope and Cures. *IMF Staff Papers, 45,* 559–594.

Thierer, A. D. (1998). A Five-Point Checklist for Successful Electricity Deregulation Legislation (1169). The Heritage Foundation, Backgrounder #1169.

Whaples, R. (2006). Do Economists Agree on Anything? Yes. *The Economists' Voice, 3*(9), 1–6.

Williamson, J. (1989). What Washington Means by Policy Reform. In J. Williamson (Ed.), *Latin American Readjustment: How Much has Happened.* Washington, DC: Institute for International Economics.

CHAPTER 3

Conditionality and Structural Adjustment Programmes

3.1 The Tyranny of Conditionality and SAPs

In 1952 a decision was taken by the IMF Executive Board to introduce conditionality, requiring any country seeking financial assistance to abide by certain conditions. These conditions are embodied in structural adjustment programmes (SAPs), which borrowing countries have to meet in order that their requests for loans are approved or the funds that have already been approved are released. Typically, structural adjustment programmes are based on laissez-faire free-market economics and the ideology of neoliberalism, in the spirit of the ten commandments of the Washington Consensus or variants thereof.

Until the early 1980s, IMF conditionality largely focused on macroeconomic policies. Following the expansion of the scope of the IMF operations to cover low-income and transition countries, the guidelines on conditionality were revised in 2002. In March 2009, the IMF revised the conditionality framework with the objective of preventing and resolving crises. In 2012, the Executive Board discussed staff papers reviewing the guidelines on conditionality, emphasising the need to "draw lessons from previous crises and provide better targeted and flexible lending". Unfortunately, none of these lessons was the big lesson learned from the global financial crisis: that laissez-faire free-market policies could bring about devastation. Even the former chairman of the Federal Reserve, Alan Greenspan, admitted once that he had learned that lesson—not the IMF though. Rather than learning this lesson, the IMF reconsidered debt limits

© The Author(s) 2019
I. A. Moosa, N. Moosa, *Eliminating the IMF*,
https://doi.org/10.1007/978-3-030-05761-9_3

policy as an integral component of conditionality. In June 2015, a new policy was put in place, encompassing all public debt rather than only external public debt, integrating treatment of concessional and non-concessional external debt, and providing closer links between public debt vulnerabilities and the use and specification of public debt conditionality.

According to the IMF (2016) conditionality is described as follows:

> Conditionality in its broad sense covers both the design of IMF-supported programs—that is, the macroeconomic and structural policies—and the specific tools used to monitor progress toward the goals outlined by the country in cooperation with the IMF. Conditionality helps countries solve balance of payments problems without resorting to measures that are harmful to national or international prosperity. At the same time, the measures are meant to safeguard IMF resources by ensuring that the country's balance of payments will be strong enough to permit it to repay the loan. All conditionality under an IMF-supported program must be either critical to the achievement of macroeconomic program goals or for monitoring implementation, or necessary for the implementation of specific provisions under the IMF's Articles of Agreement and policies thereunder.

The most bizarre statement in this description is that "conditionality helps countries solve balance of payments problems without resorting to measures that are harmful to national or international prosperity". Conditionality invariably leads to riots as the cost of living soars, and this cannot be conducive to national prosperity. As for "international prosperity", which invariably means prosperity in "western" countries, it is not clear how subsidising flour in a poor African country affects the prosperity of the people living in Australia. However, if "international prosperity" refers to the prosperity of multinationals, then surely cheap bread in a poor country is bad. If a country chooses not to comply with conditionality by refusing to privatise public assets, such an action will have a negative impact on the profit and hence the prosperity of multinationals—for this act the country must be punished.

Compliance with conditionality is enforced by disbursing funds in instalments linked to demonstrable policy actions, which is an act of brutal blackmail. The IMF periodically assesses the progress of its programme and determines whether or not modifications are necessary for achieving the programme's objectives. The Fund monitors compliance with the policy commitments agreed upon with the borrowing country and observes indicators, including the following: (i) actions that the borrowing country agrees to take *before* the approval of financing (the release of funds); (ii) quantitative performance criteria pertaining to macroeconomic indicators; (iii) indicators of progress towards the achievement of the objectives of a programme; and (iv) structural benchmarks, which refer to "reform" measures needed to accomplish the underlying objectives that are critical to achieve the stated goals. Expanding the scope of conditionality (from monetary, fiscal and exchange policies into fields that had previously been largely outside the IMF's purview) has led to a decline in the rate of compliance.

SAPs are designed to make the economies of the borrowing countries more market oriented by following the ten commandments of the Washington Consensus, and variants thereof. Typically, a SAP contains a set of "stabilisation policies" that are either related or exactly identical to the commandments of the Washington Consensus. The components that are exactly identical (which will not be discussed again here) include deregulation, privatisation and trade liberalisation. Others are modifications or restatements of the corresponding principles of the Washington Consensus. These will be dealt with one by one in the following sections.

3.2   Currency Devaluation

Currency devaluation, which is linked to the Washington Consensus principle of maintaining competitive exchange rates (the fifth commandment), is prescribed to reduce or eliminate a balance of payments deficit. To start with, let us see who has got the deficit, which is shown in Fig. 3.1. The preaching countries, the UK and the US, come on top in terms of the current account deficit as a percentage of GDP. This is again preaching what is not practised. The UK and the US have by far greater external deficits than those of some impoverished countries such as Nepal, Madagascar and Papua New Guinea. It is more of a puzzle because the US and the UK have significant surpluses from the export of arms, thus contributing to the impoverishment of already impoverished countries.

That aside, currency devaluation works only under very strict conditions that are rarely met in reality. The process is supposed to work as follows: (i) devaluation leads to a lower foreign currency price of exports and a higher domestic currency price of imports; (ii) changes in prices lead to changes in quantities, a rise in the quantity of exports and a fall in the quantity of imports; and (iii) higher export revenue and lower import expenditure lead to a reduction in the trade deficit. This sounds straightforward, perhaps too good to be true, but for this process to work the following assumptions must hold:

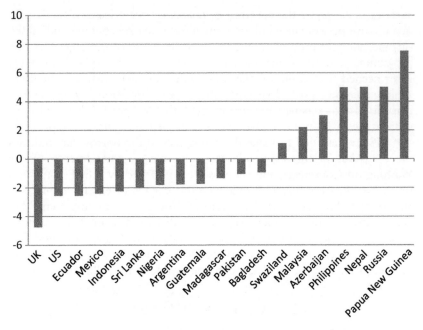

Fig. 3.1 Current account balance as a percentage of GDP

1. Full (or at least high) pass-through effect from the exchange rate to the foreign currency price of exports and the domestic currency price of imports.
2. The volume of exports must rise more proportionately than the rise in price to produce a net increase in export revenue.
3. The volume of imports must decline more proportionately than the fall in price, so that there is a net decline in import expenditure.
4. The domestic supply of exports is infinitely elastic, in the sense that any increase in foreign demand can be met by utilising excess capacity—that is, exporters must be capable and willing to accommodate the increase in foreign demand.
5. Prices and volumes are not affected by factors other than the exchange rate, or at least no offsetting effects operate in the opposite direction.

For the process to work, the demand for exports and imports must be elastic—this is the Marshall-Lerner condition that the sum of the elasticities of demand for exports and imports is greater than one. For the process to work, the currency of invoicing must be the currency of the underlying country, which is typically not the case for developing countries that tend to use the US dollar as a currency of invoicing. For the process to work, the external demand for domestic products must be strong, which is unlikely to be the case now that countries are experiencing anaemic growth. And for the process to work, competitiveness must depend on prices only or predominantly, which is not always the case as perceived quality and consumer loyalty are other determining factors.

Ironically the prime preaching country (the US) has been blaming its trade deficit with China on an alleged undervaluation of the Chinese currency, thus urging China to revalue the yuan. This is an intrusion on China's economic policy and its sovereign right to choose the exchange rate regime it deems appropriate for its economy (which is allowed by the IMF in accordance with the Jamaica Accord). Like devaluation, revaluation is unlikely to work for seven reasons: (i) distribution mark-ups and importers' profit margins, (ii) producers' profit margins, (iii) the currency of invoicing, (iv) inelastic demand for Chinese exports, (v) inelastic supply of US exports, (vi) the offsetting effects of other factors such as inflation and growth, and (vii) the deficit is an American problem, resulting from excess consumption. These propositions are illustrated in detail by Moosa (2013).

In reality the motivation for urging the borrowing countries to devalue their currencies, as in the Washington Consensus, is to make it cheaper for multinationals to acquire assets and operate in an environment characterised by low running costs, particularly the cost of labour. A significant amount of work has been done on the relation between foreign direct investment (FDI) and the exchange rate. Goldberg (2009), for example, says the following:

> When a currency depreciates, meaning that its value declines relative to the value of another currency, this exchange rate movement has two potential implications for FDI. First, it reduces that country's wages and production costs relative to those of its foreign counterparts. All else equal, the country experiencing real currency depreciation has enhanced "locational advantage" or attractiveness as a location for receiving productive capacity investments.

Aliber (1970, 1971) put forward a hypothesis to explain FDI in terms of the relative strength of various currencies. This hypothesis postulates that firms belonging to a country with a strong currency tend to invest abroad, whereas those belonging to a country with a weak currency do not have such a tendency. In other words, countries with strong currencies tend to be sources of FDI while countries with weak currencies tend to be host countries or recipients of FDI.

Currency devaluation is beneficial for multinationals but not for the devaluing developing countries. While it is unlikely to have a positive effect on the balance of payments, it leads to imported inflation. As the prices of imported goods rise, so does the cost of living, and the standard of living of the people living in the devaluing country declines. It is recommended only because the IMF is more concerned with the profit of multinationals than the welfare of the people it is supposed to help. Stiglitz (2002) suggests that the IMF "was not participating in a conspiracy, but it was reflecting the interests and ideology of the Western financial community".

3.3   AUSTERITY

The objective behind the prescription of austerity is to reduce the budget deficit, by cutting public spending (including subsidies) and raising taxes. Austerity is therefore linked to the Washington Consensus commandments of fiscal policy discipline, reducing public spending and tax "reform". Stiglitz (2002) argues that prescribing fiscal austerity is effectively reverting to Herbert Hoover's economics whereby austerity is imposed when the economy is in deep recession. Under these conditions, fiscal tightness makes things worse.

The casualties of austerity are often social programmes, particularly spending on health and education, which end up hurting economic growth. For example, Rowden (2009) suggests that austerity has hindered investment in public health infrastructure. The consequences, according to Rowden, have been dilapidated health infrastructure, inadequate numbers of health personnel, and demoralising working conditions that have fuelled the "push factors" driving the brain drain of nurses migrating from poor countries to rich ones, all of which have undermined public health systems and the fight against Human Immunodeficiency Virus/Acquired Immune Deficiency Syndrome (HIV/AIDS) in developing countries. The *New York Times* has found evidence indicating that the rise in Tuberculosis

(TB) is linked to IMF loans (Bakalar 2008). Hertz (2004) suggests that conditionality and SAPs retard social stability and lead to an increase in poverty in recipient countries.

We will say more about the effect of IMF operations on social expenditure, but what we want to do here is to elaborate on what seems to be a contradiction between cutting the budget deficit and reducing the corporate tax rate. For the Washington preachers, there is no contradiction. The twisted economic logic is that cutting the corporate tax rate is conducive to growth, which generates a higher level of tax revenue, leading to improvement in the budgetary position. The same twisted logic is used to justify cutting taxes for the rich.

Supply-side economists contend that tax reductions stimulate economic growth to such a degree that tax revenue would rise rather than fall. However, little empirical evidence is available to support this hypothesis. In a study of the Joint Committee on Taxation (2005) that examined the economic effects of reducing marginal tax rates, it is suggested that "growth effects eventually become negative ... because accumulating federal government debt crowds out private investment". The study concludes that "lowering marginal tax rates is likely to harm the economy over the long run if the tax reductions are deficit financed".

This is not the conclusion reached by Aaron et al. (2004), who found that "historical evidence shows no clear correlation between tax rates and economic growth" and that "comparisons across countries confirm that rapid growth has been a feature of both high- and low-tax nations". Allard and Lindert (2006) undertook an extensive examination of economic performance in developed countries since the 1960s, analysing the relation between economic performance and government policy across a wide range of areas, including tax policy, spending policy and regulatory policy in product and labour markets. They also controlled for various economic and demographic factors that could be expected to affect economic performance. Their results show that at levels of taxation at or even significantly above those now seen in the US, a higher ratio of tax revenue to GDP leads to an improvement in economic performance. They explained this result by noting that the additional revenues raised by higher-tax countries are frequently used to undertake growth-promoting activities like investment in public education, infrastructure and public health.

Kogan (2003) evaluated the claims that the Bush tax cuts of 2001 would boost growth and found "little support for claims made by Administration officials and other proponents of these tax cuts that either the 2001 tax cut or the new growth package would generate substantial improvements in long-term economic growth", that "these tax cuts would have only a small effect on the economy over the long term", and that "the effect is as likely to be negative as positive". In 2003, 450 economists, including ten Nobel Prize laureates, signed a statement opposing the Bush tax cuts (available at http://www.epi.org/page/-/old/stmt/2003/statement_signed.pdf). They expressed the view that economic growth had not been sufficient to generate jobs and prevent unemployment from rising, but that "the tax cut plan proposed by President Bush is not the answer to these problems". The statement made it clear that "passing these tax cuts will worsen the long-term budget outlook, adding to the nation's projected chronic deficits" and that "this fiscal deterioration will reduce the capacity of the government to finance Social Security and Medicare benefits as well as investments in schools, health, infrastructure, and basic research". Moreover, it was suggested that "the proposed tax cuts will generate further inequalities in after-tax income".

3.4   RESTRUCTURING OF FOREIGN DEBT

Debt restructuring is a process that allows a private or public company, or a sovereign country facing cash flow problems and financial distress, to reduce and renegotiate its delinquent debts to improve or restore liquidity so that it can continue its operations. Debt restructuring, which involves a reduction of debt and an extension of payment terms, is usually a less expensive alternative to bankruptcy. It can be done by using debt-equity swap, whereby creditors agree to cancel some or all of the debt in exchange for equity in the company or public assets. Haley (2017) describes sovereign debt restructuring as follows:

> Sovereign debt restructurings can be messy. In the most egregious cases, they result in protracted negotiations during which the debtor country loses access to capital markets, forcing an abrupt adjustment of consumption, investment and government expenditures. This reduction in "absorption" and the resulting compression of imports simply reflect the fact that the balance of payments accounts must "balance". But this adjustment can lead to output losses and higher unemployment that frays the social fabric.

Debt restructuring involves negotiations between a strong party (the creditor) and a weak party (the debtor). Indebted developing countries typically mortgage their assets to creditors. With debt restructuring, more concessions are given to creditors and more public assets are mortgaged. If restructuring involves debt-equity swap, the creditor might end up owning public assets that could not be obtained otherwise. Recall what happened during the disastrous privatisation programme in Russia under the "fore-sighted leadership" of Boris Yeltsin, the darling of the west. By the middle of 1994, 70% of the economy was privatised in an orgy of corruption that created the Russian oligarchy. In the run-up to the 1996 presidential election, which Yeltsin won with the help of foreign meddling, he initiated a "loans-for-shares" programme that transferred ownership of some natural resource enterprises to powerful businessmen in exchange for loans to help with the government budget. The scheme worked to the benefit of the oligarchs (and Yeltsin himself) at the expense of the people at large (unless we consider the ownership of Chelsea Football Club by a Russian citizen to be a good enough compensation for the people at large). Debt restructuring is unlikely to work to the benefit of the debtor country.

3.5   FREE-MARKET PRICING

Free-market pricing is related to the second commandment of the Washington Consensus, which requires the elimination of food subsidies and raising the prices of public services. The rationale is to obey the market because it is always right. A free market implies a structure whereby the production, distribution and pricing of goods and services are co-ordinated by the market forces of supply and demand, unhindered by regulation. A free market is the opposite of a regulated market, where the government intervenes through regulatory measures in the setting of prices and determination of the production and distribution of goods and services. An economy that is composed entirely of free markets is referred to as a free-market economy, a situation that is alternatively called laissez-faire. The problem with the description of a free market as an unregulated market is defining the extent of "unregulation". Some free marketeers maintain that a free market is not compromised by government action to enforce contracts and property rights. Others suggest that even these areas must be left to the market itself to be resolved through negotiation between those who are directly involved. For some, even the US does not have a free-market economy (e.g., Allison 2012).

The tendency to follow the rules dictated by the market can be justified on the following grounds: (i) a free market acts as a co-ordinator of independent decisions of millions of people concerning production and consumption; (ii) it performs the function of co-ordinating decisions without anyone having to understand how it works; (iii) it determines a distribution of the total income it generates; and (iv) it creates a product life cycle, leading to regular emergence of new products. Free marketeers contend that the market is the best co-ordinator, that it is a producer of growth, that it decentralises power and thus involves less coercion, and that market-determined prices are related to costs. The formal case for a free market is that it would lead to an optimal allocation of resources and hence efficiency, in the sense that no one can be made better off without simultaneously making someone else worse off. According to free marketeers, the beauty of markets is that they have no conscience, meaning that they are impartial (but they are also tyrants).

The origin of the concept of a free market is traced by Gray (2009) to mid-nineteenth-century England where a "far-reaching experiment in social engineering" was conducted. The objective, according to Gray, was to "free economic life from social and political control" by instituting the idea of free market, which required the breaking up of the socially-rooted markets that had existed in England for centuries. Gray, who is a critic of free-market ideology, argues that "the free market created a new type of economy in which prices of all goods, including labour, changed without regard to their effects on society".

The economist who more than anyone else popularised the concept of free market and sold it successfully to politicians (and to the public at large through popular media) was Milton Friedman, who went as far as declaring that "underlying most arguments against the free market is a lack of belief in freedom itself" (Friedman 1962). He also articulated the proposition that economic freedom is a precondition for political freedom. Freedom of expression, he argued, is not possible when the means of production are under government control and individuals lack the economic means to sustain themselves and their points of view. Sirico (2012) echoes this view by warning that "you cannot have freedom without a free economy".

Another prominent advocate of the notion of free market is Friedrich von Hayek, who established "Neoliberal International", a transatlantic network of academics, businessmen, journalists and activists. The rich backers of the scheme funded a series of think-tanks that worked on the refinement and promotion of the ideology. Among the backers were the American Enterprise Institute, the Heritage Foundation, the Cato Institute, the Institute of Economic Affairs, the Centre for Policy Studies and the Adam Smith Institute. The backers also financed academic positions and departments, particularly at the universities of Chicago and Virginia.

Friedrich von Hayek is quoted by Petsoulas (2001) as saying that market economies allow "spontaneous order"—that is, "a more efficient allocation of societal resources than any design could achieve". According to this view, sophisticated business networks operating in market economies are formed to produce and distribute goods and services throughout the economy. This network, the argument goes, has not been designed, but emerged as a result of decentralised individual economic decisions. Supporters of the idea of spontaneous order trace their views to the concept of the "invisible hand" proposed by Adam Smith in *The Wealth of Nations*. Smith (1776) pointed out that one does not get one's dinner by appealing to the brotherly love of the butcher, the farmer or the baker. Rather, one appeals to their self-interest and pays them for their labour. Free marketeers claim that, due to the number and complexity of the factors involved, spontaneous order is superior to any order that does not allow individuals to make their own choices as to what to produce, what to buy, what to sell and at what prices. They further believe that any attempt to implement central planning will result in more disorder and a less efficient production and distribution of goods and services. The problem with this argument is that the alternative to a free-market economy is not necessarily central planning, socialism, communism or fascism.

Critics of the free-market ideology include those who reject markets entirely in favour of a planned economy, as well as those who wish to see market failure regulated to various degrees or supplemented by government intervention. The opponents of free markets contend that the government at times has to intervene to ensure competition in large and important industries. While its supporters argue that only a free market can create healthy competition, and therefore more business and reasonable prices, opponents say that a free market in its purest form may produce the opposite of the desired outcome. It is plausible to suggest that the merging of companies into giant corporations or the privatisation of public enterprises and national assets often results in monopolies (or oligopolies) requiring government intervention to force competition and reasonable prices.

Critics of the free-market ideology dispute the claim that free markets create perfect competition, or even boost market competition in the long run. They assert that government intervention is necessary to remedy market failure that is held to be an inevitable result of absolute adherence to free-market principles. This is the central argument of those who advocate a mixed market system that has an element of government oversight while being free at the base. Ubel (2009) uses behavioural economics to advocate restrictions on free markets. The market, he thinks, has its place—he even quotes Adam Smith on the benefits of the division of labour and agrees enthusiastically with the underlying principles. However, he suggests that "market fanatics have gone too far". And, unlike Clark and Lee (2011) who claim that markets promote morality, Falk and Sczech (2013) suggest that markets erode morals.

Critics of laissez-faire see unregulated markets as an impractical ideal or as a rhetorical device that puts the concepts of freedom and anti-protectionism at the service of vested wealthy interests, allowing them to attack labour laws and the rules providing protection for the working classes. Because no national economy in existence manifests the ideal of a free market as theorised by the true believers, some critics of the concept consider it to be a fantasy falling outside the bounds of reality, contending that markets fail in the sense that they cannot achieve an optimal allocation of resources. Apart from that, they justify intervention on the grounds of equity, protecting individuals from others, protecting individuals from themselves (paternalism) and honouring social obligations such as jury duty and voting.

The free-market ideology has been dealt a big blow by the global financial crisis because deregulation is seen as a major cause of the crisis. A large number of books attacking the free-market ideology were published in the aftermath. Indeed there was (and still is) renewed interest not only in the work of Keynes but also in the work of Marx (*Das Kapital* was reprinted in huge volumes to meet surging demand). Mason (2018) opines on the meaning of Marxism today, arguing that "it is not Marx's vision of historical forces but his surprising faith in the individual that makes him a key thinker for the age of automation".

In the aftermath of the crisis, Gray (2009) wrote the following:

> In the era of the free market, now fast slipping from memory, the past hardly existed. Only the present had any reality, and it was being constantly refashioned and made new. New industries, new careers, new lives were continuously created, and discarded according to market imperatives. Grandiose doctrines sprang up to support the belief that the free-market capitalism that had been adopted in a handful of countries would prevail over every economic system.

Gorton (2010) discredits the invisible hand by writing:

Economists view the world as being the outcome of the "invisible hand", that is, a world where private decisions are unknowingly guided by prices to allocate resource efficiently. The credit crisis raises the question of how it is that we could get slapped in the face by the invisible hand.

He goes on to argue that it was private decisions made over a long time that created the shadow banking system, which was vulnerable to a banking panic. For Cohan (2009), the crisis was caused by a combination of "risky bets, corporate political infighting, lax government regulation and truly bad decision making". Motivated by the crisis, Stiglitz (2010) argues for a restoration of the balance between government and markets, suggesting that the (free-market) system is broken and that it can be fixed only by "examining the underlying theories that have led us into this new bubble capitalism". Fox (2009) documents an admission by Alan Greenspan in a Congressional hearing held in October 2008 that the free-market ideology that guided him for 40 years was not working.

Martinez (2009) contends that the proposition that the activities related to distributing resources and economic growth are better left to the "invisible hand" seems "tragically misguided in the wake of the 2008 market collapse and bailout". He goes on to describe how "the flawed myth of the 'invisible hand' distorted our understanding of how modern capitalist markets developed and actually work". Martinez draws from history to illustrate not only that political processes and the state are instrumental in making capitalist markets work but that there would be no capitalist markets or wealth creation without state intervention. Likewise, Harcourt (2011) argues that "our faith in 'free markets' has severely distorted American politics".

It is bewildering that belief in the healing power of the free market is still firm despite the devastation inflicted by the global financial crisis on the world economy. Some free marketeers go as far as blaming the global financial crisis on regulation rather than deregulation. For example, Allison (2012) points out that "financial services is a very highly regulated industry, probably the most regulated industry in the world"—hence "it is not surprising that a highly regulated industry is the source of many of our economic problems". The fact of the matter is that if, prior to the crisis, there were adequate regulations of leverage, liquidity, underwriting standards and the trading of over the counter (OTC) derivatives, the crisis would not have happened or at least would have been less devastating.

The fact of the matter is that government intervention in economic activity is needed, particularly when something big goes wrong. A person cutting himself shaving does not need the intervention of a surgeon, as the body can heal itself from such a minor mishap. However, a person who gets shot and survives the shooting needs the intervention of a surgeon—otherwise, he will die.

3.6   IMPROVING GOVERNANCE AND FIGHTING CORRUPTION

The Washington preachers tell developing countries to reduce the level of corruption that mostly takes the shape of exchanging a favour for an envelope containing a few thousand dollars. In the preaching countries, bankers defraud the general public of billions of dollars and get away with it—in fact they are rewarded with big bonuses for defrauding people. London has become the world capital of financial fraud, and New York is not that far behind.

Transparency International (2015) suggests that "corruption in the banking sector has manifested itself in many scandals involving money laundering, rate rigging and tax evasion, all of which undermine the public's trust in financial institutions". Excessive risk taking with other peoples' money is fraud. As Dewatripont and Freixas (2012) put it, "it has been noted that risk taking is intrinsically involved in the business of banking and that this can lead to unethical conduct at the expense of the public interest". The extent of corruption on Wall Street is best described by Snyder (2010) as follows:

> If you ask most Americans, they will agree that the financial system is corrupt. It is generally assumed that just like most politicians, most big bankers are corrupt by nature. But the truth is that the vast majority of Americans have no idea just how corrupt the US financial system has become. The corruption on Wall Street has become so deep and so vast that it is hard to even find the words to describe it. It seems that the major financial players will try just about anything these days—as long as they think they can get away with it. But in the process they are contributing to the destruction of the greatest economic machine that the planet has ever seen.

Kaufman (2009) describes as a myth the proposition that "corruption is a challenge mainly for public officials in developing countries and that it is unrelated to the current global crisis". He argues strongly that "corruption is not unique to developing countries, nor has it declined on average". The difference may be trivial: in a developing country a corrupt official may be paid for his services by receiving an envelope full of cash; in a developed country, the payment is more subtle—for example, the promise of a lucrative job in the future.

The 2014 *Global Fraud Study*, conducted by the Association of Certified Fraud Examiners, reveals that the Australian financial sector experienced a greater number of fraud incidents than any other sector (ACFE 2014). Fraud includes scandals perpetrated by financial planners, mortgage fraud, insider trading and kickbacks. Jones (2015) argues that "the Australian banking sector is dominated by corrupt organizations that also run banks on the side, supported by a craven, supplicant media and political establishment". Strubel (2014) describes the financial sector as the "greatest parasite in human history". Drum (2012) thinks that fraud in the financial sector is getting worse, suggesting that one reason why "the financial sector is still trading at less than book value" is that "the number of investors who trust the banks is now zero". Kaufman (2009) suggests that the study of corruption ought to include acts that may be legal in a strict narrow sense but where the rules of the game have been bent, arguing that this broader view of corruption would make the scale of fraud in the financial sector even greater than what it appears to be. The situation is succinctly described by Schechter (2010), who suggests that "the 'F Word' (for fraud) is back in polite conversation on Wall Street" and that "fraud and financial crime are slowly becoming part of the debate over what must be done to restore confidence in what has so plainly been a confidence game".

In a conference on finance and society held in May 2015, Brooksley Born declared that the dangers of fraud have only grown since the global financial crisis (Martens and Martens 2015). She said the following:

> The power and influence of the financial sector threatens a continuation of the regulatory capture that contributed to the financial crisis. Financial firms, too often, have significant say in the appointment of high regulatory officials. The tendency of some former government officials to obtain highly lucrative positions in the financial sector after leaving government may well act as an inducement to those remaining in government to serve the interest of the financial sector rather than those of the public.

Corruption is a cause of financial instability and crises. The results of a 1986 Federal Deposit Insurance Corporation (FDIC) survey show that criminal misconduct by insiders was a major contributing factor in 45% of bank failures (Sprague 1986). The last three major crises (the savings and loan crisis, the subprime crisis and the global financial crisis) were caused predominantly by greed-driven fraud and corruption. This is not to say that there was a single cause for the global financial crisis, but the facts on the ground imply that corruption must come on top.

Wray (2011) puts a very strong case for the role of fraud in the global financial crisis, which he characterises as a solvency rather than liquidity crisis. However, he recognises a run on liquidity, which he describes as a "refusal to refinance one's fellow crooks", adding that "criminal enterprise always relies on trust, and when that breaks down, war breaks out". He refers to a small-time bank robber, Willy Sutton, who responded to the question as to why he robbed banks by saying, "because that's where the money is". Wray describes the global financial crisis as "the biggest scandal in human history", but then he qualifies his statement:

> It is apparent that fraud became normal business practice. I have compared the home finance food chain to Shrek's onion: every layer was not only complex, but also fraudulent, from the real estate agents to the appraisers and mortgage brokers who overpriced the property and induced borrowers into terms they could not afford, to the investment banks and their subsidiary trusts that securitized the mortgages, to the credit ratings agencies and accounting firms that validated values and practices, to the servicers and judges who allow banks to steal homes, and on to CEOs and lawyers who signed off on the fraud. To say that this is the biggest scandal in human history is an understatement. And the fraudsters are still running the institutions.

One form (perhaps the worst and most damaging form) of corruption is regulatory capture. Baxter (2011) presents a working definition of capture as follows: "regulatory capture [is] present whenever a particular sector of the industry, subject to the regulatory regime, has acquired persistent influence disproportionate to the balance of interests envisaged when the regulatory system was established". George Stigler once said the following: "as a rule, regulation is acquired by the industry and is designed and operated primarily for its benefits" (Stigler 1971). Regulatory capture, according to Kaufman (2009), is not readily observable and any action motivated by capture can be justified otherwise, which makes it "one neglected dimension of political corruption". Capture occurs when powerful companies (or individuals) bend the rules for their private benefit by using high-level bribery, lobbying or influence peddling. Banks and major financial institutions fit this description more than other firms. Green and Nader (1973) suggest that capture is enhanced by the exchange of personnel, arguing that "a kind of regular personnel interchange between [regulatory] agency and industry blurs what should be a sharp line between regulator and regulatee, and can compromise independent regulatory judgment". Baxter (2011) emphasises the "revolving door" as follows:

> As both our need for expert regulators and the skill of regulators increase, the doors between regulators and the industry will spin faster. If we are to engage in technical regulation at all, this is not only unavoidable, but sometimes even desirable. But revolving doors are also dangerous: many current examples vividly highlight the unseemly appearance, if not reality, of an incestuous relationship between regulators and industry that must surely risk fostering an improper influence of industry over the regulators.

Regulatory capture played a big role in the advent of the global financial crisis. According to Kaufman (2009), capture was the main reason for the systemic failure of oversight, regulation and disclosure in the financial sector. Furthermore, regulatory capture is the cause of what Johnson and Boone (2010) call the "doomsday cycle". The implicit and explicit subsidies granted to financial institutions deemed too-big-to-fail (TBTF) or systemically important financial institutions (SIFIs) encourage excessive risk taking and moral hazard, which would eventually result in loss-making bets. Regulation is imposed to discourage excessive risk taking, but the regulators are captured by loss-making financial institutions. When those institutions fail, the regulators come to the rescue through bailout (stealing taxpayers money), bail-in (stealing depositors money) or/and quantitative easing (printing money and giving it away at zero interest rate). These are the subsidies that encourage excessive risk taking—and so the process repeats itself for the benefit of the financial oligarchy at the expense of taxpayers, depositors and the middle class at large.

In an interview on his article "Why isn't Wall Street in Jail" Matt Taibbi (2011) describes the Securities and Exchange Commission (SEC) as a classic case of regulatory capture. The SEC has also been described as "an agency that was set up to protect the public from Wall Street, but now protects Wall Street from the public" (Bauder 2011). On 17 August 2011, Taibbi reported that in July 2001, a preliminary fraud investigation against Deutsche Bank was stymied by a former SEC enforcement director, who began working as general counsel for Deutsche Bank in October 2001. Darcy Flynn, an SEC lawyer and the whistleblower who exposed this case, revealed that for 20 years, the SEC had been routinely destroying documents related to thousands of preliminary inquiries that were closed rather than proceeding to formal investigation.

Corruption is rampant in the City of London. Roberto Saviano, the Italian investigative journalist, is quoted by Carrier (2016) as saying that "the financial services industry based in the City of London facilitates a system that makes the UK the most corrupt nation in the world". He adds:

> If I asked what is the most corrupt place on Earth, you might say it's Afghanistan, maybe Greece, Nigeria, the south of Italy. I would say it is the UK. It's not UK bureaucracy, police, or politics, but what is corrupt is the financial capital. Ninety per cent of the owners of capital in London have their headquarters offshore.

In reference to the secretive offshore markets of Jersey and the Caymans, Saviano describes them as the "access gates to criminal capital in Europe and the UK is the country that allows it". These offshore financial centres serve what he calls "criminal capitalism", and he argues that most financial companies that reside offshore are exactly like the mafia and organised crime that do not abide by the rule of law.

Likewise, Logan (2018) puts forward reasons why "London's status as a global centre for financial corruption is no accident", mentioning in particular government inaction on money laundering that has allowed Russian "kleptocrats and human rights abusers" to hide "dirty money". Aldrick (2016) describes the City as a "slush fund for dirty cash" where accountants, lawyers and bankers play enabler for drug barons, terrorists and venal politicians, flushing vast fortunes through London's property, art and, above all, financial markets. Alexandroni (2007) talks about corruption by saying the following:

> We may associate the word corruption with Russian oligarchs and African republics run by venal government officials, yet according to the watchdog, Transparency International, the world capital of dirty money is not Moscow or Mogadishu. It is London.

When "western" countries talk about rampant corruption in developing countries they measure corruption in terms of the corruption perception index (CPI)—out of 179 countries, the 80 lowest ranked are largely poor African and Asian countries, whereas the UK comes in 13th position. However, the CPI does not measure supply-side corruption as crooked officials could not loot their countries on a massive scale without easy access to global financial centres willing to be the custodians of their money, and no financial centre plays a bigger role in supply-side corruption than London. Alexandroni (2007) quotes Laurence Cockcroft, director of Transparency International UK, as saying that "the City of London has become the number-one home for the fruits of corruption". While the government is aware of the situation, no action is taken because any such action would "stifle economic growth". After all, "who needs manufacturing industry when we have the City"?

3.7   Enhancing the Rights of Foreign Investors Vis-à-Vis National Law

The policy prescription of enhancing the rights of foreign investors vis-à-vis national law is consistent with the tenth commandment of the Washington Consensus. There have been cases where foreign investors demand compensation for the host government's decisions to introduce new environmental and public health measures, as well as tax increases, changes to the regulatory regime governing utility pricing and alleged mistreatment by the judiciary. Foreign investors' claims under investment treaties are not always successful. The ability of foreign investors to frame plausible multi-million dollar claims against a wide range of host government actions—and the fact that these claims are adjudicated through a system of private arbitration—has made investment treaties controversial.

Some mixed empirical evidence is available on the impact of investment treaties on FDI. For example, an UNCTAD (2014) review of 35 published and unpublished studies on the impact of investment treaties found that the majority suggest that investment treaties do have some positive impact of FDI inflows, while a significant minority reach the opposite conclusion. Focusing exclusively on published studies, Bonnitcha et al. (2017) reach essentially the same conclusion, while emphasising the significant differences in methodological quality between various studies. They also note that, among studies that do find a positive impact of investment treaties on FDI, different studies reach contradictory findings about the circumstances in which investment treaties are likely to have a positive impact on FDI.

The rationale for the ultra-generous treatment of foreign investors rests on two assumptions: (i) additional FDI inflows are beneficial from the perspective of the host country, which is not always the case; and (ii) the absence of a level playing field between domestic and foreign investors. Some studies use legal methodologies to determine the extent to which investment treaties grant preferential rights to foreign investors. It is undisputed that investment treaties grant substantive rights to foreign investors that go well beyond guarantees of non-discrimination. Examples include guarantees of "fair and equitable treatment" and the protection of the so-called umbrella clause. However, academics disagree about whether such guarantees are equivalent to, or more generous than, the legal protections commonly provided to investors within the legal systems of more advanced economies (e.g., Johnson and Volkov 2013; Kleinheisterkamp 2014; Parvanov and Kantor 2012).

Other studies use empirical methodologies to test the hypothesis that, in the absence of investment treaties, foreign investors suffer from discrimination in host countries vis-à-vis their domestic competitors. The results obtained from this strand of research suggest that foreign investors are not subject to regulatory or judicial treatment in host countries that is inferior to the treatment of equivalent domestic competitors (Aisbett and McAusland 2013; Aisbett and Poulsen 2016), casting doubt on the proposition that host governments treat foreign investors more poorly than they treat their domestic competitors.

The fact of the matter is that the claims that foreign investors receive inferior treatment can be used to make a case for putting foreign investors above the law, particularly in developing countries. The perpetrators of the December 1984 Bhopal disaster got away with mass murder, the killing of up to 8000 Indian villagers by "chemical weapons". The main cause of the disaster was underinvestment in safety, which created a dangerous working environment. Specific factors include the filling of tanks beyond recommended levels, poor maintenance and switching off safety systems to save money.

3.8   Financialisation

Financialisation, as an integral part of SAPs, comes under various labels such as creating new financial institutions and the opening of domestic stock markets for the purpose of boosting the stability of investment and supplementing FDI. While a sound financial sector is essential, the financialisation of the economy could turn out to be a very bad idea, particularly if it is taken too far. Krishnan (2016) considers the implementation of neoliberal policies and the acceptance of neoliberal economic theories in the 1970s to be the root of financialisation, with the financial crisis of 2007–2008 as one of the ultimate results.

Financialisation is a term that describes the dominance of the financial sector over other sectors of the economy, including manufacturing industry and agriculture. It refers to "the increasing importance of financial markets, financial motives, financial institutions, and financial elites in the operation of the economy and its governing institutions, both at the national and international levels" (Epstein 2002). Komlik (2015) describes financialisation simply as "the ascendancy of finance", suggesting that it represents "the capturing impact of financial markets, institutions, actors, instruments and logics on the real economy, households and daily life". Phillips (2006) views financialisation as "a process whereby financial services, broadly construed, take over the dominant economic, cultural, and political role in a national economy". Financialisation represents regulatory and political capture. David Stockman, a former director of the Office of Management and Budget, once described financialisation as "corrosive", arguing that it had turned the economy into a "giant casino" where banks skim an oversize share of profits (Bartlett 2013).

Prior to the advent of the global financial crisis, economists examined the effect of financial development on economic growth and development. In this strand of literature the relation between financial development and economic growth is examined by using a variety of econometric techniques applied to cross-sectional, time series and panel data (e.g., King and Levine 1993a, b; Levine 1997, 2003; Rajan and Zingales 1998; Choe and Moosa 1999; Levine et al. 2000; Beck and Levine 2004; Beck et al. 2000, 2005). By and large, the results of these studies indicate the presence of a positive long-run association between financial development and economic growth. This finding can be rationalised on the grounds that a well-developed financial market enhances growth by providing credit, the means of payment and a variety of financial instruments that can be used to conduct financial operations. However, the global financial crisis has led to a reconsideration of this conclusion because the crisis demonstrated that a malfunctioning financial system can exert negative effects, both directly and indirectly, and becomes a drag on the real sector of the economy. This phenomenon is sometimes known as the "finance curse", which is typically associated with excessively large financial sectors (e.g., Shaxson and Christensen 2013).

Numerous studies have demonstrated the adverse consequences of financialisation, particularly the retardation of growth and intensification of inequality, which are arguably related in the sense that inequality itself retards growth. For example, Bartlett (2013) suggests that "Financialisation is also an important factor in the growth of income inequality, which is also a culprit in slow growth". Cushen (2013) explores the means whereby the workplace outcomes associated with financialisation render employees insecure and angry. Black (2011) lists the ways in which the financial sector harms the real economy, describing its functions as "the sharp canines that the predator state uses to rend the nation". The adverse effects of financialisation have been widely recognised as being mostly related to the accumulation of debt, which leads to a diversion of increasing portions of the financial resources of the corporate and household sectors to debt service.

Financialisation has adverse macroeconomic consequences because it makes the financial system weaker by boosting leverage, opacity, complexity and spillover effects within and outside financial institutions, and by accelerating debt deflation (Sinapi 2014). Furthermore, the dominance of finance fuels capital asset price inflation as suggested by Bellofiore (2013). Financialisation has a depressive effect on productive investment, consumption and aggregate demand. For example, Lavoie (2012) associates financialisation with the development of a consumption-led accumulation regime fuelled by increasing household debt as households strive to compensate for their stagnating purchasing power. Given that financial crises cause subsequent recessions and that financialisation leads to a bigger and more unstable financial sector, the link between financialisation and output becomes conspicuous. According to the IMF (2009), recessions associated with financial crises last on average 18 months longer than other recessions and take almost three years to go back to pre-recession output levels. According to Crotty (1990, 2009) the financial sector has grown so fast that it poses a threat to the growth of the real economy by generating endogenous financial instability and exerting a depressive impact on the real sector.

As a summary, the literature suggests that financialisation has adverse effects on living standards, capital accumulation, consumption, productivity, aggregate demand, value added, the distribution of income, employment, wages, tax revenue, asset price inflation, financial stability, and the opacity and complexity of the financial sector. It is intuitive to suggest that some of these effects imply adverse consequences for aggregate output and economic growth. Other mechanisms include competition with the real sector for resources, the brain drain inflicted by the financial sector on the real sector, the Dutch disease explanation and the dominance of a mentality of trading for short-term gains.

Stock markets are not necessary for investment, but they provide a means of transferring money from the poor to the rich. They do not create any value added. However, they provide the means whereby foreign investors can dispose of their holdings in local companies quickly as in the "hot money cycle" envisaged by Stiglitz (Plasat 2001). A big financial sector facilitates corruption, which is convenient for predatory foreign investors.

3.9   Arguments Against Conditionality and SAPs

Conditionality is justified on the grounds that it is a means to ensure that the borrowing country will be able to repay the IMF and that it will not attempt to solve its balance of payment problems in a way that would have an adverse effect on the international economy. However, it is not obvious how a small impoverished country seeking financial assistance could behave in such a way as to have adverse consequences for the world economy. Another justification is related to moral hazard, which arises when a country behaves in such a way as to maximise its own utility to the detriment of others when it does not bear the full consequences of its action. In the case of IMF lending, moral hazard is controlled by attaching conditions to the loan rather than the provision of collateral.

Yet another justification is that conditionality is a means for reassuring that the borrowed funds are used for the stated purpose, typically to rectify macroeconomic and structural imbalances. The underlying idea is that when the borrowing country uses the funds for the stated purpose, it will be in a position to repay the IMF, thereby ensuring that the resources will be available to support other members of the Fund. Is this not exactly the argument used by common loan sharks? The IMF seems to think that governments of developing countries favour political gain over national economic interests by engaging in rent-seeking practices to consolidate political power rather than address crucial economic issues. The Fund uses the observation that borrowing countries have had a very good track record for repaying their loans, implying that IMF lending does not impose a burden on creditor countries.

Khan and Sharma (2001) suggest that the discussion of the nature and merits of IMF conditionality has a long history and that the issue has gained renewed attention, with questions raised about whether or not the conditions imposed by the IMF on borrowing countries have been too intrusive, and whether or not the design and implementation of IMF conditionality has undermined country ownership of adjustment programmes aimed at correcting macroeconomic imbalances. They use concepts and results from the finance literature to suggest that some form of conditionality is present in all borrower-lender relationships—the key to the ability to borrow is the ability to pledge income back. They quote Carlos Diaz-Alejandro (1984) as saying that conditionality stems from a "patron-beneficiary" relationship between the IMF and the borrowing country. Another proposition put forward by Khan and Sharma is that finance considerations provide justification for IMF conditionality—hence they cast doubt on the view expressed by Killick (1997) that IMF conditionality should be the exception rather than the rule.

Khan and Sharma (2001) use historical conjecture to justify IMF conditionality, arguing that the conditionality attached to sovereign lending has a long history. Ferguson (1998) recalls a case from 1818 when Prussia, effectively bankrupted by the Napoleonic wars, approached Nathan Rothschild for a loan. From the onset of negotiations, Rothschild argued that any loan would have to be secured by a mortgage on Prussian royal domains guaranteed by the Stande (parliament) of the domains concerned. Khan and Sharma (2001) also suggest that the modern model for conditional lending to sovereign governments in the absence of collateral is considered by many to be the Turkish agreement of 1881—known as the "Decree of Mouharrem"—that was implemented after the Turkish government defaulted on its foreign debt in 1875. The League of Nations attached strict conditionality in its adjustment programmes, or the "reconstruction schemes" of the 1920s. These conditions included maintenance of fiscal equilibrium and monetary discipline, as well as currency reform.

It is ironic that Nathan Rothschild is viewed as a role model as he made a fortune by financing two warring parties. He was a financial genius, recognising a long time ago that lending to governments is a profitable business as governments can always tax people to repay their debt, which is why lending to governments does not require collateral. However, lending with collateral is more merciful than lending with IMF conditionality because the former means that the borrower loses the collateral only in the case of default. Lending with IMF conditionality means that the borrowing country loses public assets even if it does not default.

Conditionality has been criticised on several grounds. It undermines domestic political institutions and stability. The recipient governments sacrifice policy autonomy in exchange for funds, which can lead to public resentment of the local leadership for accepting and enforcing the IMF conditions. A country may be compelled to accept conditions that it would not accept if it were not for a financial crisis. Political instability can result from more leadership turnover as political leaders are replaced in electoral backlashes. In June 2018, the Jordanian prime minister was replaced after months of riots in opposition to IMF demands. Conditionality is also a common cause for reducing government services, rising unemployment and social instability. Stiglitz (2002) argues that conditionality is not just the typical requirements that anyone lending money might expect the borrower to fulfil in order to ensure that the money will be paid back. Rather, he argues that "conditionality refers to more forceful conditions, ones that often turn the loan into a policy tool". Dreher (2009) suggests that IMF conditionality is ineffective and that the evidence does not support the proposition that conditionality makes success more likely.

SAPs are designed to deal, by using standard tools that are applied to every country irrespective of local circumstances, with poor governance, excessive government spending, excessive government intervention in economic activity and too much state ownership. According to Hertz (2004), SAPs aggravate poverty in recipient countries. Joseph Stiglitz criticises SAPs, arguing that by converting to a more monetarist approach, the purpose of the IMF is no longer valid, as it was designed to provide funds for countries to carry out Keynesian reflations (Stiglitz 2002; Friedman 2002). SAPs threaten the sovereignty of national economies because a foreign organisation dictates the recipient country's economic policy when policy formulation is or should be a sovereign right. There is no reason why a foreign organisation cares more for the people of a country than its elected (or unelected) government to the extent that the foreign organisation formulates better policies than the local government.

The IMF economists always recommend ideologically driven policies without having any knowledge of unique domestic circumstances, which may make the recommended policies difficult to carry out, unnecessary or even counterproductive. According to Stiglitz (2002), the economists of the IMF recommend a "one-size-fits-all" policy based on their academic training, which focuses on economic models with unrealistic assumptions about how real-life economies work. They do not specialise in the economies of the countries whose policies they oversee, they do not live in those countries, but rather in Washington, and they have little appreciation for the political circumstances under which governments operate.

SAPs are viewed by some post-colonialists as the modern procedure of colonisation (McGregor 2005). Minimising the ability of the government to regulate the domestic economy opens the door for multinational companies to come in and extract cheap resources. Jahn (2005) argues that while agreements with the IMF are "voluntary", they are to all intents and purposes "imposed", and that the "voluntary" signatures do not signify consent to the details of the agreement, but rather desperate need. Structural programmes are intended to change the cultural, economic and political constitution of a target country without the consent of the government or the people of that country.

The policies typically take the form of "shock therapy" designed to move the economy from one extreme to another. In May 2003, the IMF recommended the transformation of the economy of occupied Iraq to pure capitalism overnight by removing, with immediate effect, all subsidies, charging market prices for government-provided goods and services, and privatising everything under the sun. The same shock therapy was used in Russia in the early 1990s with disastrous effects. The policies are implemented all at once, rather than in an appropriate sequence. According to Stiglitz (2002), this is a result of the IMF's "market fundamentalism", a blind faith in the free market that ignores the facts on the ground. Privatisation is advocated in the name of efficiency, but the cost is invariably massive redundancies. Stiglitz (2002) points out that if a country's unemployment programme and other social safety nets are not sufficiently developed, those losing their jobs will have no way to support their families.

SAPs are "hush-hush" endeavours. The IMF is not open to criticism or public oversight when it forces the implementation of its policies, leading to arrogance and lack of connection to the reality on the ground. For example, Stiglitz (2002) contends that agreements between the IMF and borrower countries are kept secret from the general public. Officials of the borrowing countries typically feel powerless to question the IMF's policies, believing that just to ask a question would be viewed by the IMF as a challenge to its authority and jeopardise the loans it was offering. A great lack of trust therefore characterises relations between the Fund and its borrowers, as the public and governments of borrower countries are kept out of the loop on the decisions that would shape their economic future.

Guimond (2007) examines the implementation of SAPs in post-conflict countries and the propositions that they lead to rising political tensions, economic instability or recessions, increased poverty and inequality, and even conflict. A quantitative study of 43 post-conflict settings reveals on the surface that the relationship between SAP indicators and conflict renewal is strongly negative. On the other hand, the results are much more ambiguous when intervening factors are examined more closely. The results then show that when SAPs are implemented most successfully, conflict renewal is more likely. They also show that a declining inflation rate (a central component of SAPs) does not boost the stability of the peace process, and may even contribute to instability. Given that horizontal inequality and dependence on certain natural resources are strongly associated with higher risk of conflict renewal, SAPs become a contributing factor to conflict renewal because they typically lead to higher levels of inequality and dependence on natural resources.

3.10   CONCLUDING REMARKS

Is there any connection between Shakespeare and the IMF? Anyone would answer this question in the negative, at least because Shakespeare died long before the emergence of the IMF. However, there is a connection: an element of *The Merchant of Venice* resembles to a large extent IMF conditionality. So, let us remind ourselves of events in Shakespeare's *Merchant of Venice*.

Antonio, a Venetian merchant, is asked by his friend Bassanio for a loan that he needs desperately. Antonio agrees, but he is unable to make the loan because his own money is invested in a number of ships that are still at sea. He suggests that Bassanio obtain a loan from a money lender and name him as the guarantor. Antonio and Bassanio approach Shylock for a loan, notwithstanding the fact that Shylock holds a long-standing grudge against Antonio for criticising the practice of lending money at exorbitant interest while he (Antonio) offers interest-free loans. Surprisingly, Shylock agrees to give Bassanio an interest-free loan. However, a conditionality provision is added to the loan contract—that Shylock will be entitled to a pound of Antonio's own flesh in the case of default. Despite Bassanio's warnings, Antonio agrees.

As the loan approaches maturity, rumours surface that Antonio's ships have been wrecked, in which case the latter will default. It turns out that Antonio has indeed lost his ships, which means that he has to satisfy the conditionality provision by surrendering one pound of flesh. Shylock ignores pleas to show mercy, insisting that the pound of flesh is rightfully his. Bassanio offers Shylock twice the money due to him, but Shylock demands the collection of the bond as agreed upon.

Although the story ends on a happy note due to the wisdom of a legal expert, what we are interested in here is to compare the conditionality of the IMF and the conditionality of Shylock. If anything, the conditionality of Shylock is less severe as the pound of flesh would be collected only in the case of default. IMF conditionality compels the borrowing country to privatise, deregulate, liberalise and starve its people to death before the release of funds. If Shylock behaved like the IMF, he would demand his pound of flesh as a precondition for granting the loan, releasing the funds only after taking delivery of the pound of flesh.

REFERENCES

Aaron, H. J., Gale, W. G., & Orszag, P. R. (2004). Meeting the Revenue Challenge. In M. Rivlin & I. Sawhill (Eds.), *Restoring Fiscal Sanity*. Washington, DC: Brookings Institution Press.

ACFE. (2014). Report to the Nations on Occupational Fraud and Abuse. http://www.acfe.com/rttn/docs/2014-report-to-nations.pdf

Aisbett, E., & McAusland, C. (2013). Firm Characteristics and Influence on Government Rule-Making: Theory and Evidence. *European Journal of Political Economy, 29*, 214–235.

Aisbett, E., & Poulsen, L. (2016). Are Aliens Mistreated? The Relative Treatment of Foreign Firms in Developing Countries. www.atw2017.qut.edu.au/program/documents/Emma%20Aisbett.pdf

Aldrick, P. (2016, May 11). For Fantastically Corrupt Practices, Look No Further Than the City of London. *The Times.*

Alexandroni, S. (2007, October 4). London Tops the Poll Observations on Corruption. *New Statesman.*

Aliber, R. Z. (1970). A Theory of Direct Foreign Investment. In C. P. Kindleberger (Ed.), *The International Corporation: A Symposium*. Cambridge, MA: MIT Press.

Aliber, R. Z. (1971). The Multinational Enterprise in a Multiple Currency World. In J. H. Dunning (Ed.), *The Multinational Enterprise*. London: Allen & Unwin.

Allard, G. J., & Lindert, P. H. (2006, August). Euro-Productivity and Euro-Job Since the 1960s: Which Institutions Really Mattered. NBER Working Papers, No. 12460.

Allison, J. A. (2012). *The Financial Crisis and the Free Market: Why Capitalism is the World Economy's Only Hope*. New York: McGraw-Hill.

Bakalar, N. (2008, July 22). Rise in TB Is Linked to Loans From I.M.F. *New York Times*.

Bartlett, B. (2013, June 11). Financialisation as a Cause of Economic Malaise. *New York Times*.

Bauder, D. (2011, 17 February). Gary Aguirre Major Source in Taibbi Blockbuster. http://www.sandiegoreader.com/weblogs/financial-crime-politics/2011/feb/17/gary-aguirre-major-source-in-taibbi-blockbuster/#

Baxter, L. G. (2011). Capture in Financial Regulation: Can we Channel it Toward the Common Good? *Cornell Journal of Law and Public Policy, 21*, 175–200.

Beck, T., & Levine, R. (2004). Stock Markets, Banks, and Growth: Panel Evidence. *Journal of Banking and Finance, 28*, 423–442.

Beck, T., Levine, R., & Loayza, N. (2000). Finance and the Sources of Growth. *Journal of Financial Economics, 58*, 261–300.

Beck, T., Demirgüç-Kunt, A., & Maksimovic, V. (2005). Financial and Legal Constraints to Firm Growth: Does Size Matter? *Journal of Finance, 60*, 137–177.

Bellofiore, R. (2013). Two or Three Things I Know about her: Europe in the Global Crisis and Heterodox Economics. *Cambridge Journal of Economics, 37*, 497–512.

Black, W. (2011, May 25). How the Servant Became a Predator: Finance's Five Fatal Flaws. http://www.huffingtonpost.com/william-k-black/how-the-servant-became-a_b_318010.html

Bonnitcha, J., Poulsen, L., & Waibel, M. (2017). *The Political Economy of the Investment Treaty Regime*. Oxford: Oxford University Press.

Carrier, D. (2016, May 29). Roberto Saviano: London is Heart of Global Financial Corruption. *The Guardian*.

Choe, C., & Moosa, I. A. (1999). Financial System and Economic Growth: The Korean Experience. *World Development, 27*, 1069–1082.

Clark, J. R., & Lee, D. R. (2011). Markets and Morality. *Cato Journal, 31*, 1–25.

Cohan, W. D. (2009). *House of Cards*. London: Allen Lane.

Crotty, J. (1990). Owner-Manager Conflict and Financial Theories of Investment Instability: A Critical Assessment of Keynes, Tobin, and Minsky. *Journal of Post Keynesian Economics, 12*, 519–542.

Crotty, J. (2009). Structural Causes of the Global Financial Crisis: A Critical Assessment of the 'New Financial Architecture'. *Cambridge Journal of Economics, 33*, 563–580.

Cushen, J. (2013). Financialisation in the Workplace: Hegemonic Narratives, Performative Interventions and the Angry Knowledge Worker. *Accounting, Organizations and Society, 38,* 314–331.

Dewatripont, M., & Freixas, X. (Eds.). (2012). *The Crisis Aftermath: New Regulatory Paradigms.* London: Centre for Economic Policy Research.

Diaz-Alejandro, C. F. (1984, January 7–February 9). IMF Conditionality: What Kind? *PIDE Tidings.*

Dreher, A. (2009). IMF Conditionality: Theory and Evidence. *Public Choice, 141,* 233–267.

Drum, K. (2012, December 19). Corruption and Fraud in the Financial Industry Get Worse and Worse. http://www.motherjones.com/kevin-drum/2012/12/corruption-and-fraud-financial-industry-get-worse-and-worse

Epstein, G. A. (2002). Financialisation, Rentier Interests, and Central Bank Policy. Working Paper, Department of Economics and Political Economy Research Institute (PERI) University of Massachusetts, Amherst.

Falk, A., & Szech, N. (2013). Morals and Markets. *Science, 340,* 707–711.

Ferguson, N. (1998). *The House of Rothschild: Money's Prophets 1798–1849.* New York: Viking Press.

Fox, J. (2009). *The Myth of the Rational Market.* New York: Harper Business.

Friedman, M. (1962). *Capitalism and Freedom.* Chicago: University of Chicago Press.

Friedman, B. M. (2002). Globalization: Stiglitz's Case. New York Review of Books. http://www.nybooks.com/articles/2002/08/15/globalization-stiglitzs-case/

Goldberg, L. S. (2009). Exchange Rates and Foreign Direct Investment. In K. A. Reinert & R. S. Rajan (Eds.), *The Princeton Encyclopedia of the World Economy.* Princeton: Princeton University Press.

Gorton, G. B. (2010). *Slapped by the Invisible Hand: The Panic of 2007.* Oxford: Oxford University Press.

Gray, J. (2009). *False Dawn: The Delusions of Global Capitalism* (Rev. ed.). London: Granta Publications.

Green, M., & Nader, R. (1973). Economic Regulation vs. Competition: Uncle Sam the Monopoly Man. *Yale Law Journal, 82,* 876.

Guimond, M. F. (2007). Structural Adjustment and Peacebuilding: Road to Conflict or Peace? Working Paper, Development Program Initiative.

Haley, J. A. (2017). Sovereign Debt Restructuring: Bargaining for Resolution. CIGI Papers No. 124.

Harcourt, B. E. (2011). *The Illusion of Free Markets: Punishment and the Myth of Natural Order.* Cambridge, MA: Harvard University Press.

Hertz, N. (2004). *The Debt Threat.* New York: Harper Collins.

IMF. (2009). *World Economic Outlook.* Washington DC: International Monetary Fund.

IMF. (2016). Conditionality. http://www.imf.org/en/About/Factsheets/ Sheets/2016/08/02/21/28/IMF-Conditionality

Jahn, B. (2005). Kant, Mill, and Illiberal Legacies in International Affairs. *International Organization, 59*, 177–207.

Johnson, S., & Boone, P. (2010, February 22). The Doomsday Cycle. *Vox.*

Johnson, L., & Volkov, O. (2013). Investor-State Contracts, Host-State "Commitments" and the Myth of Stability in International Law. *American Review of International Arbitration, 24*, 361–415.

Joint Committee on Taxation. (2005, March 1). Macroeconomic Analysis of Various Proposals to Provide $500 Billion in Tax Relief, JCX-4-05. http://www.house.gov/jct/x-4-05.pdf

Jones, E. (2015, March 31). The Australian Banking Sector: Predatory and Unaccountable. https://independentaustralia.net/business/business-display/the-australian-banking-sector-predatory-and-untouchable,7539

Kaufman, D. (2009, January 27). Corruption and the Global Financial Crisis. *Forbes.*

Khan, M. S., & Sharma, S. (2001). IMF Conditionality and Country Ownership of Programs. IMF Working Papers, No. 01/142.

Killick, T. (1997). Principals, Agents and the Failings of Conditionality. *Journal of International Development, 9*, 483–495.

King, G. R., & Levine, R. (1993a). Finance and Growth: Schumpeter Might be Right. *Quarterly Journal of Economics, 108*, 717–737.

King, G. R., & Levine, R. (1993b). Finance, Entrepreneurship and Growth. *Journal of Monetary Economics, 32*, 1–30.

Kleinheisterkamp, J. (2014). Financial Responsibility in European International Investment Policy. *International and Comparative Law Quarterly, 63*, 449–476.

Kogan, R. (2003, March 3). Will Tax Cuts Ultimately Pay for Themselves? Center on Budget and Policy Priorities.

Komlik, O. (2015, January 31). What is Financialisation? Marxism, Post-Keynesianism and Economic Sociology's Complementary Theorizing. *Economic Sociology and Political Economy.* http://economicsociology.org/2015/01/31/what-is-Financialisation-marxism-post-keynesianism-and-economic-sociologys-complementary-theorizing/

Krishnan, G. (2016, May 15). Exposing The IMF and World Bank—Organizations that are Systematically Controlling and Crippling the World Economy Through Neoliberalism. https://www.linkedin.com/pulse/exposing-imf-world-bank-organizations-controlling-economy-krishnan

Lavoie, M. (2012). Financialisation, Neo-Liberalism, and Securitization. *Journal of Post Keynesian Economics, 35*, 215–233.

Levine, R. (1997). Financial Development and Economic Growth: Views and Agenda. *Journal of Economic Literature, 35*, 688–726.

Levine, R. (2003). More on Finance and Growth: More Finance, More Growth? *Federal Reserve Bank of St. Louis Review, 85,* 31–46.

Levine, R., Loayze, N., & Beck, T. (2000). Financial Intermediation and Growth: Causality and Causes. *Journal of Monetary Economics, 46,* 31–77.

Logan, C. (2018, May 21). 4 Key Reasons Why London's Status as a Global Centre for Financial Corruption is no Accident. www.commonspace.scot

Martens, P., & Martens, R. (2015, May 7). Brooksley Born Still Telling the Uncomfortable Truths about Wall Street. *Wall Street on Parade.* http://wall-streetonparade.com/2015/05/brooksley-born-still-telling-the-uncomfort-able-truths-about-wall-street/

Martinez, M. A. (2009). *The Myth of the Free Market: The Role of the State in a Capitalist Economy.* Sterling: Kumarian Press.

Mason, P. (2018, May 4–10). The Meaning of Marxism Today. *New Statesman,* 27–31.

McGregor, S. (2005). Structural Adjustment Programmes and Human Well-Being. *International Journal of Consumer Studies, 29,* 170–180.

Moosa, I. A. (2013). The Magnificent Seven: Reasons why Revaluation of the Yuan will not Work. *International Journal of Economics, 7,* 113–131.

Palast, G. (2001, April 29). IMF's Four Steps to Damnation. *The Guardian.* https://www.theguardian.com/business/2001/apr/29/business.mbas

Parvanov, P., & Kantor, M. (2012). Comparing US Law and Recent US Investment Agreements: Much More Similar than you might Expect. In K. Sauvant (Ed.), *Yearbook on International Investment Law and Policy 2010–2011.* Oxford: Oxford University Press.

Petsoulas, C. (2001). *Hayek's Liberalism and its Origins: His Idea of Spontaneous Order and the Scottish Enlightenment.* London: Routledge.

Phillips, K. (2006). *American Theocracy: The Peril and Politics of Radical Religion, Oil, and Borrowed Money in the 21st Century.* London: Viking.

Rajan, R., & Zingales, L. (1998). Financial Dependence and Growth. *American Economic Review, 88,* 559–586.

Rowden, R. (2009). *The Deadly Ideas of Neoliberalism: How the IMF has Undermined Public Health and the Fight Against AIDS.* New York: Zed Books.

Schechter, D. (2010, April 2). Financial Fraud and the Economic Crisis, Global Research. http://www.globalresearch.ca/financial-fraud-and-the-economic-crisis/18444

Shaxson, N., & Christensen, J. (2013). *The Finance Curse: How Oversized Financial Centres Attack Democracy and Corrupt Economies.* London: Tax Justice Network.

Sinapi, C. (2014). The Role of Financialisation in Financial Instability: A Post-Keynesian Institutionalist Perspective. Working Paper, Burgundy School of Business. Geopoliticki Casopis (Special Issue on World Economic and Social Crisis), 207–232.

Sirico, R. A. (2012). *Defending the Free Market: The Moral Case for a Free Economy.* Washington, DC: Regnery Publishing.

Smith, A. (1776) The Wealth of Nations, New York: The Modern Library (Random House).

Snyder, M. (2010, April 13). 11 Examples of How Insanely Corrupt the US Financial System Has Become. http://endoftheamericandream.com/archives/11-examples-of-how-insanely-corrupt-the-u-s-financial-system-has-become

Sprague, I. H. (1986). *Bailout: An Insider's Account of Bank Failures and Rescues.* New York: Basic Books.

Stigler, G. (1971). The Theory of Economic Regulation. *Bell Journal of Economics and Management Science, 2,* 3–21.

Stiglitz, J. (2002). *Globalization and its Discontents.* New York: Norton.

Stiglitz, J. (2010). *Free Fall: America, Free Markets, and the Sinking of the World Economy.* New York: Norton.

Strubel, B. (2014, March 31). The Financial Sector is the Greatest Parasite in Human History. *New Economic Perspectives.* http://neweconomicperspectives.org/2014/03/financial-sector-greatest-parasite-human-history.html

Taibbi, M. (2011, February 16). Why Isn't Wall Street in Jail? *Rolling Stone.*

Transparency International. (2015). Incentivising Integrity in Banks. Working Paper. http://www.transparency.org/whatwedo/publication/incentivising_integrity_in_banks

Ubel, P. A. (2009). *Free Market Madness: Why Human Nature is at odds with Economics—and Why it Matters.* Cambridge, MA: Harvard Business Press.

UNCTAD. (2014). The Impact of International Investment Agreements on Foreign Direct Investment: An Overview of Empirical Studies 1998–2014. http://investmentpolicyhub.unctad.org/Upload/Documents/unctad-web-diae-pcb-2014-Sep%2024.pdf

Wray, L. R. (2011, August). Lessons We Should Have Learned from the Global Financial Crisis but Didn't, Levy Economics Institute of Bard College. Working Paper No. 681.

CHAPTER 4

The IMF as an Instigator of Riots and Civil Unrest

4.1   THE IMF RIOTS

Riots have erupted throughout history to protest against, amongst other things, escalating cost of living. The term "food riots" is used to describe protests against rising food prices, which can be caused by a number of factors including harvest failures, faulty food storage, transport-related problems, speculation on food prices, hoarding, poisoning of food and pest attacks. Brinkman and Hendrix (2011) provide an overview of the link between food insecurity and violent conflict, addressing both traditional and emerging threats to security and political stability. They discuss the effects of food insecurity on several types of conflict, and the political, social and demographic factors that may exacerbate these effects. Bellemare (2014) produces empirical evidence showing that for the period 1990–2011, rising food prices have led to escalating social unrest.

When rising food prices, among other adverse consequences, are caused by IMF-prescribed policies, we have on our hands an "IMF riot". The term "IMF riots" was coined to describe waves of protests witnessed by developing countries throughout the 1980s and 1990s, when many of them were in crisis and had to resort to borrowing from the IMF. Invariably, those countries sought relief in IMF borrowing but ended up in deeper crises than what they had started with because the conditionality associated with IMF lending involves austerity measures and the abolition of subsidies, leading to skyrocketing prices of food, fuel and other essential items characterised by low price elasticities of demand.

© The Author(s) 2019
I. A. Moosa, N. Moosa, *Eliminating the IMF*,
https://doi.org/10.1007/978-3-030-05761-9_4

Marshall (2014) defines the term "IMF riots" by referring to "dozens of nations around the world that experienced waves of protests in response to the IMF/World Bank programs of the 1980s and 1990s, which plunged them into crisis through austerity measures, privatisation and deregulation all enforced under so-called structural adjustment programs". Typically these measures affect the poor segment of the society and aggravate income and wealth inequality. The so-called trickle-down effect, that what is good for the rich is good for the whole society, provides no salvation for the poor, simply because it is a myth.

With particular reference to the IMF (and World Bank), Woodroffe and Ellis-Jones (2000) describe "protests and demonstrations organised by the southern poor", which are "aimed at policies that hurt their livelihoods and, in some cases, undermine the democratic foundations of their countries". They add the following:

> Teachers, civil servants, priests, farmers, students, doctors, trade-union activists, indigenous peoples and women's groups have called on their governments to halt the introduction of economic reforms which have bypassed their national democratic institutions, and have been foisted on them by the IMF and World Bank. These are poor people, in a desperate situation, who are striving for respect, dignity and a sense of pride in their lives and countries. Their voices deserve to be heard. But they're not. Developing countries are still locked into a dependant relationship with the international financial institutions and donor governments. Despite the rhetoric of poverty reduction, debt relief and economic stabilisation, these countries must still implement liberalisation policies which hurt the poor.

Ryan (1998) refers to "frequent correlation" between the IMF adjustment programmes and "political instability and unrest", using this association to explain why "the International Monetary Fund (IMF) has long remained one of the most controversial institutions on the world stage". While the IMF may be viewed favourably as representing a key source of financial survival, it is, in Ryan's words, a "hated and powerful economic overseer akin to a thuggish loan shark". Ryan remarks that "it is the latter more pejorative image of the IMF that seems to resonate more clearly with the general public throughout Africa, Latin America, Asia and the Middle East". The negative image of the IMF can be attributed largely to "the social and political costs associated with economic adjustment".

The arguments put forward by Woodroffe and Ellis-Jones (2000) and Ryan (1998) are shared by Marshall (2014), who refers to "social unrest and revolution emanating from the world's major international financial institutions like the IMF and World Bank, as well as the world's major consulting firms that provide strategic and investment advice to corporations, banks and investors around the world". With respect to the IMF, Marshall (2014) argues that "as IMF austerity programs spread across the globe, poverty followed, and so too did protests and rebellion". He cites figures showing that between 1976 and 1992, there were 146 protests against IMF-sponsored programmes in 39 different countries around the world characterised by "violent state repression of the domestic populations". He further writes the following:

> These same programs by the IMF and World Bank facilitated the massive growth of slums, as the policies demanded by the organizations forced countries to undertake massive layoffs, privatization, deregulation, austerity and the liberalization of markets—amounting, ultimately, to a new system of social genocide. The new poor and displaced rural communities flocked to cities in search of work and hope for a better future, only to be herded into massive urban shantytowns and slums.

Oxfam (2002) attributes the food crisis in southern Africa to the failure of IMF-designed agricultural policies. These policies are designed without carrying out a full assessment of their likely impact on poverty and food security. These policies, according to Oxfam (2002), aim to replace inefficient and corrupt state intervention in agriculture with private sector provision. To deal with this issue, Oxfam makes the following recommendations: (i) mandatory impact assessments, (ii) ensuring food security, (iii) a role for governments, (iv) delivery of food aid, (v) suspension of debt repayments, (vi) supporting the "development box" and (vii) putting an end to dumping.

The IMF riots, however, are not limited to poor countries, as Marshall (2014) refers to "protests against austerity and structural adjustment measures—erupting over the past three years in Greece, Spain, Portugal and elsewhere in the EU". Ponticelli and Voth (2017) examine the link between austerity and social unrest in 28 European countries over the period 1919–2008, measuring the level of social unrest in terms of five major indicators: riots, anti-government protests, general strikes, political assassinations and attempted revolutions. They detect a "clear and positive statistical association between expenditure cuts and the level of unrest" and conclude that spending cuts "create the risk of major social and political instability". Needless to say, some of the episodes examined by Ponticelli and Voth (2017) have nothing to do with the IMF, but since the IMF-recommended policies invariably induce massive cuts in expenditure, these policies produce civil unrest. Even worse, expenditure cuts as recommended by the IMF typically target the poor segment of the population as emphasis is laid upon the removal of subsidies and the introduction of significant cuts in social expenditure.

4.2   THE STIGLITZ FOUR-STEP PROCESS

Joseph Stiglitz, a Nobel Prize-winning economist, blew the whistle on the World Bank's and IMF's policies in countries around the world, in the process losing his job as the World Bank's chief economist and subsequently smeared for exposing malpractices and exploitation on a grand scale. Greg Palast, who interviewed Stiglitz for *The Guardian* in 2001, describes the events associated with the firing of Stiglitz as follows (Palast 2001):

> It was like a scene out of Le Carré: the brilliant agent comes in from the cold and, in hours of debriefing, empties his memory of horrors committed in the name of an ideology gone rotten. But this was a far bigger catch than some used-up Cold War spy. The former apparatchik was Joseph Stiglitz, ex-chief economist of the World Bank. The new world economic order was his theory come to life. The World Bank fired Stiglitz two years ago. He was not allowed a quiet retirement: he was excommunicated purely for expressing mild dissent from globalisation World Bank-style.

In his interview with Palast, Stiglitz described the four-step process that any country seeking financial assistance must go through. The eruption of riots in response to the IMF's operations is "step 3.5" in his characterisation of the Fund's and Bank's operations, which he described meticulously in his interview with Palast. Step 1 is the privatisation of state-owned industries and assets, particularly electricity and water companies, a process that involves a significant element of corruption. On this issue, Stiglitz accused local politicians of shaving a few billion off the sale price of national assets in return for "the promise of 10% commissions paid to their Swiss bank accounts". Stiglitz also accused the US government of being complicit in scandals like these, saying that "the US government knew it", with particular reference to the 1995 Russian sell-off. The view of the US Treasury, as expressed by Stiglitz, was the following: "This was great, as we wanted Yeltsin re-elected. We DON'T CARE if it's a corrupt election". While the US-backed oligarchs associated with Yeltsin stripped Russia's high-value public assets, the national output was cut nearly in half and a super power all of a sudden turned into an impoverished developing country where people could not afford to bury their dead. Is it surprising then that "western" countries and the Russian oligarchs hate Putin? Is it not ironic that so much fuss is made these days about Russian "meddling" in the US election (and the French and the British and the election of every so-called western democracy)?

The second step, which involves a "hot money cycle", is capital market liberalisation or deregulation. This is meant to allow capital flows to come in and go out without any impediment. The problem, according to Stiglitz, is that "the money often simply flows out", because at any sign of trouble, capital outflows intensify dramatically in a matter of days. The process is described as a "hot money cycle" because capital comes in for speculation in real estate and currency, then flees at the first sign of trouble. At this point, the IMF prescribes higher interest rates to stem the outflow of capital, and when interest rates go as high as 80%, the economy is wrecked. The IMF prescribes policies that typically have adverse consequences, and when conditions deteriorate, the Fund prescribes further policies that make the situation even worse. Anyone with any measure of sound judgement will tell us that it is senseless to expect an arsonist to put out a fire that he (or she) started.

Step 3 involves the so-called market-based pricing, as the elimination of subsidies forces the prices of food and other essential consumer items upwards. This is followed by step 3.5, an IMF-caused riot that Stiglitz describes as "peaceful demonstrations dispersed by bullets, tanks and tear gas". Riots cause further capital flight, which is good for predatory foreign investors who can then pick off remaining assets at fire-sale prices (and be praised for helping those in need). Stiglitz believes that "this process is always anticipated by the IMF and World Bank, which have even noted in various internal documents that their programs for countries could be expected to spark social unrest". Yet the two Washington-based institutions keep on doing business as usual, perhaps for the benefit of the predatory foreign investors.

Step 4 involves the imposition of free trade agreements (governed by the rules of the World Trade Organization) for the benefit of multinationals. Stiglitz likens the imposition of free trade to the Opium Wars, which were also about "opening markets". He expressed the following view:

> As in the nineteenth century, Europeans and Americans today are kicking down barriers to sales in Asia, Latin American and Africa while barricading our own markets against the Third World's agriculture. In the Opium Wars, the West used military blockades. Today, the World Bank [and IMF] can order a financial blockade, which is just as effective and sometimes just as deadly.

It is therefore a one-way free trade: our goods should be free to enter your markets, but not the other way round. China was bombed by the Royal Navy, because the Chinese had decided not to allow British opium to enter the country and devastate the population. It suffices to say that free trade was an invention of the British Empire and that it is free in one direction only.

Palast (2001) refers to a cache of documents marked, "confidential" and "restricted", obtained from "sources unnameable (not Stiglitz)". One of these documents is entitled a "country assistance strategy", proclaiming "an assistance strategy for every poorer nation, designed … after careful in-country investigation". According to Stiglitz, however, "investigation" involves "little more than close inspection of five-star hotels". Stiglitz went on to say that the "investigation" concludes with a meeting with a "begging finance minister", who is handed a "restructuring agreement" pre-drafted for "voluntary" signature. The begging finance minister eventually receives the "same four-step programme". The show comes to an end with smiles and firm handshakes (or what the Arabs call "nose kissing") in front of the camera. Soon afterwards, the poor people of that country start to feel the pinch and revolt because they have nothing to lose—as the proverb goes, a wet person does not fear rain.

4.3   Examples of IMF-Instigated Riots

The description of the riots presented in this section is constructed from the news items collected by Woodroffe and Ellis-Jones (2000) for the period from the mid- to late 1990s to 2000. The reports primarily comprise IMF declarations and press releases, as well as reports of disturbances and civil unrest taken from various media outlets. The news items for each country are listed in Woodroffe and Ellis-Jones (2000).

Argentina

In December 1999, a wave of strikes hit Argentina as the newly elected centre-left government attempted to "reform" labour laws in response to "discussions" with the IMF, in the process diluting the trade-union movement and undermining the rights of workers. In March 2000, the IMF approved a $7.2 billion three-year stand-by credit on the condition that the government continue with key "fiscal and structural reforms", emphasising the importance of the labour market, deregulation and the social security system. Consequently, a package of "labour reform" was passed by the Senate in April 2000, leading to violent clashes between protestors and the police in which more than 30 people were injured and about 50 arrested.

In May 2000, IMF-prescribed cuts in social security expenditure led to violent demonstrations in the Salta region, while peaceful protests turned violent after demands for unemployment benefits and severance pay were ignored by local officials who could no longer provide them. The protesters set fire to public offices before being subdued by armed riot police, leaving dozens injured and many arrested. On 31 May 2000, some 80,000 people participated in a protest organised by trade unions, the Catholic Church and some politicians. The protesters pledged "fiscal disobedience" by refusing to pay taxes as the tax rate jumped from 8% to 22%. And on 9 June 2000, a 24-hour general strike was supported by more than 7.2 million workers. This was followed on 29 August 2000 by a one-day strike by teachers and scientists, triggered by a 12% cut in wages, as prescribed by the IMF austerity measures.

In August 2018, Argentina was in the news for the same reason as the government requested an early release of a $50 billion IMF loan amid a growing economic crisis characterised by rampant inflation and currency depreciation. In a statement, the IMF said that it would "revise the government's economic plan with a focus on better insulating Argentina from the recent shifts in global financial markets, including through stronger monetary and fiscal policies and a deepening of efforts to support the most vulnerable in society". According to *The Guardian* (2018), "most Argentinians have bad memories of the IMF and blame the international lending institution for encouraging policies that led to the country's worst economic crisis in 2001". On this occasion, the government of Argentina pledged to abolish half of the government departments to please the IMF.

Bolivia

In September 1998, Bolivia received a $138 million IMF loan conditional upon the execution of plans to privatise all remaining public enterprises, including the water industry. In February 2000, the IMF granted Bolivia a $46.1 million loan in addition to $1.3 billion in debt relief, conditional upon "continued progress in the implementation of structural reforms". Those "reforms" led to a 200% hike in water prices, provoking widespread protests in December 1999 and January 2000. In February 2000, more than 1000 protesters were confronted by a similar number of riot police and soldiers. More than 175 people were injured in the encounter. In April 2000, the government declared a state of emergency, restricting civil liberties and arresting protesters while rubber bullets were replaced by real ones.

Brazil

In November 1998, the IMF offered Brazil an $18 billion stand-by loan, noting "with satisfaction" the "success of the Brazilian economy" while encouraging the government to maintain and boost privatisation programmes and enhance the liberalisation of external trade. In April 2000, a tribunal on foreign debt was held in in Rio de Janeiro, reaching the verdict that "the policies of the IMF have proved disastrous and have increased the foreign debt even more, while imposing the endless moratorium on social spending". Those who must pay the debt are identified as "children, workers in rural areas and the countryside, black people, indigenous people and the environment"—the victim is invariably the poor, the weak and the vulnerable. In September 2000, a referendum was conducted about whether or not Brazil should discontinue IMF "reforms"—one million people answered in the affirmative. On 7 September, a demonstration was organised under the banner of "Cry of the Excluded".

Colombia

In September 1999, the IMF approved a three-year credit worth $2.7 billion in support of "the government's structural reform agenda", including policies to "downsize the public sector, mainly through privatisation, and reduce public sector spending". The Fund required (read "ordered") the

Colombian government to open its economy, privatise public companies and cut back spending. In the annual review of the agreement (read "ultimatum"), the IMF welcomed the continuation of the recovery of Colombia's economic activity, "despite the challenges posed by the political and security situation". Given that the "challenges" were produced by the IMF's prescriptions, this amounts to saying that economic recovery continued despite IMF policies, but then we do not know what the IMF means by the "recovery of economic activity". On 3 August 2000, some 15,000 workers went on a 24-hour general strike to protest against IMF-imposed austerity measures that resulted in lower real wages.

Costa Rica

In 1995, Costa Rica was granted an IMF stand-by credit for $78 million on the conditions that "private sector participation in areas previously reserved for the public sector is increased" and that "a far greater role by foreign investors in areas such as electricity generation, insurance and banking is provided for". In the 1999 annual review of Costa Rica's economic programme, the IMF urged a "prompt approval of the draft legislation to open up electricity generation, telecommunications, and the insurance sector to private sector participation", describing such an action as "essential". In March 2000, a bill was introduced, outlining the IMF-prescribed privatisation of the Costa Rican Electricity Institute, leading to widespread protests. On 21 March, 40 protests took place all around the country. And on 23 March, 10,000 marchers descended on the presidential residence demanding the withdrawal of the bill.

Ecuador

In April 2000, the IMF granted Ecuador a stand-by loan of $304 million, subject to the introduction of "reforms", including dollarisation of the economy, wage restraint and the removal of subsidies. The Fund also ordered "important structural reforms in the labour market, the oil sector, and privatisation". In the first review of this agreement, the Fund was impressed by the injection of "more flexibility in the labour market", the "increased private sector participation in the economy" and the "commitment to phase out price regulations on domestic fuels and electricity". It was also noted that "a more liberal trade regime would complement these reforms".

On 7 January 2000, the government declared a state of emergency to contain growing protests as the inflation rate reached 60% while the economy shrank by 7%, conditions that constitute severe stagflation. On 15 January 2000, 40,000 Indians initiated a week of protests, against the IMF-prescribed policies. On 22 January 2000, about 3000 protesters occupied Ecuador's Congress building and surrounded the Supreme Court despite police attempts to disperse them with tear gas. In Guayaquil, Ecuador's second largest city, demonstrations become violent, leading to numerous injuries.

In March 2000, the government introduced a package of new laws to "reform" the labour market and the financial sector, boost privatisation efforts, provide oil pipeline permits and dollarise the economy. The introduction of the "reforms" was followed in May 2000 by a five-week strike organised by the National Educators Union. On the removal of fuel price subsidies, as demanded by the IMF, the government claimed that it was doing the best it could for the Ecuadorian people, and in accordance with the IMF. It therefore seems that the objective function of the Ecuadorian government was the IMF's level of satisfaction, while the constraint was the misery of the Ecuadorian people.

Further protests followed. On 15 June 2000, trade unions and church groups organised a general strike, involving more than 30,000 doctors, who staged a 72-hour sit-down protest, as well as teachers, oil workers and other public sector workers. In Quito, protesters who tried to march on the government palace were met with tear gas when one passer-by received a bullet wound. On 9 September 2000, Ecuador formally adopted the dollar as a legal tender, but the transition turned chaotic as people were left without the means to settle transactions. In a document obtained from the World Bank, it was suggested with "cold accuracy" that the adjustment programme would spark "social unrest". In the same document a prediction was made that one consequence of dollarisation was to push 51% of the population below the poverty line (Palast 2001).

It is not clear why dollarisation was recommended for Ecuador. Dollarisation, or currency substitution in general, is resorted to when the local currency is no longer capable of performing the functions of measure of value and store of value because of hyperinflation. Typically, the local currency is still used as a medium of exchange and may even be used to perform the other two functions of money when conditions get better. Surely, inflation was not as severe as it was in Zimbabwe in 2009 when a decision was taken to abandon the local currency altogether.

Honduras

On 7 June 2000, the IMF granted Honduras a $21 million loan, urging (read "telling") the government to "proceed quickly with structural reforms, especially the privatisation of telecommunications and electricity distribution and the reform of the social security and pension system". On 26 June, thousands of workers took part in a national strike demanding an increase in the minimum wage. On 27 July, thousands of secondary school teachers went on strike over unpaid wages, affecting about one million pupils. The protestors (farmers, workers and students) hampered the provision of services at hospitals and forced the closure of major highways.

Kenya

On 28 July 2000, the IMF resumed lending to Kenya, providing a $198 million loan in recognition of the government's drive to address the causes of financial instability and low growth—specifically, "stop-go macroeconomic policies" and "slow structural reform". The prescribed policies included "macroeconomic and structural reforms, civil service reform and privatisation". In April and May 2000, a peaceful demonstration in Nairobi (dubbed a debt cancellation march) called for debt relief and an end to IMF conditions. The demonstration ended in violence and the arrest of 63 protesters, including 13 nuns and 2 priests.

In August 2000, President Daniel arap Moi complained that the conditions imposed by the IMF for the new aid programme to Kenya were too harsh, and that the economic slowdown was a product of those conditions. In response, an IMF official described as "exaggeration" the complaints that the loan conditions infringed on Kenya's sovereignty. It is interesting that the word "exaggeration" is used to justify hostile action by those who refuse to admit responsibility for atrocities. For example, the number of people killed as a result of the Belgian occupation of the Congo is an exaggeration and so is the number of people who died as a result of the invasion and occupation of Iraq by the "Allied" forces. And, of course, anything that is said about the atrocities committed by the British Empire in all corners of the globe is an exaggeration.

Malawi

On 25 October 1999, the IMF granted Malawi a $10.6 million loan, conditional upon "structural reforms" needed to achieve success and in accelerating the mobilisation of committed external assistance. On 15 May 2000, protests opposing IMF conditions ended in violence. Trade unionists and human rights activists were dispersed by tear gas.

Nigeria

On 4 August 2000, the IMF approved a stand-by credit of $1031 million for Nigeria, suggesting that "an acceleration of the implementation of structural reforms is urgently needed, including to tackle serious deficiencies in the provision of power, telecommunications and petroleum that are obstacles to growth". Needless to say, the solution to these deficiencies and obstacles was "an adequate privatisation framework".

In June 2000, the government continued with the implementation of the IMF-advised fuel price hike—as a result, the country was crippled by the most serious general strike since the end of military rule. Oil workers were joined by public sector and transport staff, blocking Lagos port and highways, disrupting international and domestic flights, and closing all petrol stations. Sporadic violence was reported across Nigeria's cities, leading to several deaths. In July 2000, the Nigerian House of Representatives adopted a non-binding motion urging the government to suspend all activities pertaining to the IMF loan.

Paraguay

In the late 1990s, the IMF expressed its disappointment at the government's "lacklustre performance" resulting from "failure to implement needed structural reforms". The Fund thought that "directors underscored the importance of sequencing structural reforms appropriately while proceeding with the necessary changes in the civil service and the social security system". Concern was expressed by the Fund over the high level of the minimum wage vis-à-vis Paraguay's major trading partners, noting that the rigidities embodied in the present labour market arrangements would become more evident as the economy opened itself to world trade. In June 2000, protesters clashed with police in demonstrations against non-negotiable IMF "reforms". A 48-hour general strike was called for against the government's plans to privatise telephone, water and railway companies. In Asuncion, over 20 people were injured and five arrested as riot police attacked them with truncheons. In the east district, 300 protesters were dispersed with water cannons while two buses were set on fire at the bus terminal.

South Africa

In the IMF's view, "the extremely high level of unemployment" can be tackled by "accelerating structural reforms, increasing domestic invest- ment, attracting foreign investment, and enhancing efficiency", which requires "faster and deeper implementation of the reforms, most notably in the areas of labour market reform, trade liberalisation, and privatisa tion". On 1 February 2000, the Congress of South African Trade Unions (COSATU) initiated protests against rising unemployment and labour market "reforms". It is noteworthy that following the end of apartheid in 1994, COSATU helped introduce labour laws to protect the rights of workers. This is why attempts by the government, encouraged by the IMF, to implement wage restraint and labour flexibility were met with widespread opposition.

On 16 April 2000, Trevor Ngwane, a city councillor from the Soweto Township, said the following:

> Many of those [IMF] debts were used to buy weapons and suppress the people during apartheid. So we are paying twice for it—once with our lives, and now with an inability to fund critical social services. Instead of building health clinics the government is selling off zoos and libraries to stay in the good graces of the IMF.

Needless to say, it is not clear how those policies (particularly trade liberalisation and privatisation) can reduce unemployment. Trade liberali- sation leads to the closure, or at least a shrinking market share, of domestic firms that provide employment opportunities. Privatisation, on the other hand, invariably leads to redundancies as a result of the drive to cut costs with the ultimate objective of financing the salaries and bonuses of the new CEO and his or her inner circle.

Zambia

On 26 March 1999, the IMF granted Zambia a three-year loan worth $349 million on the condition that "the government will increase reforms in the areas of privatisation, public service, and monetary and banking supervision". On 27 July 2000, the Fund approved an additional $13.2 million loan. The loan agreement affirmed that "the [Zambian] authorities intend to pursue a prudent monetary policy and to limit the credit to public enterprises [and] complete the transition to a private-led economy, including the privatisation of the remaining public utilities and the operations of the oil sector".

On 26 April 2000, hundreds of protesters, demanding an end to IMF-prescribed policies, were dispersed by armed riot police in the capital city, Lusaka, as they tried to picket the hotel where IMF and government officials were meeting. The protesters blamed the IMF for continued poverty in their country. In August 2000, the IMF urged Zambia to "put the economy ahead of politics". IMF First Deputy Managing Director Stanley Fischer said that Zambia faced hard decisions ahead of forthcoming elections and urged the government not to put politics ahead of "economic sense". Naturally, Fischer was referring to a particular economic "sense" that the IMF operations are guided by, as he urged the government to ignore the poor, the weak and the vulnerable (or else). This is the same Stanley Fischer who in 2003 recommended the removal of all subsidies in war-torn and sanction-ravaged Iraq.

4.4   ANOTHER SET OF IMF RIOTS

In this section we present cases of anti-IMF riots in North Africa and the Middle East, spreading over the period between the 1970s and the present. These cases cover Tunisia, Morocco, Egypt, Jordan and Sudan.

Tunisia and Morocco

The cases of Tunisia and Morocco are described in detail by Seddon (1986). In December 1984, violent demonstrations started in the impoverished southwest and south of Tunisia and spread throughout the country during the first week of January. Following the introduction of measures by the Tunisian government to remove food subsidies, as part of the "economic stabilisation programme" approved by the IMF, the sudden doubling of bread prices was a crucial cause of the outbreak of protests. Naturally, government officials who struck the deal with the IMF identified a threat from "hostile elements" attempting to overthrow the government. The twisted logic here is that the victims of the conspiracy orchestrated by the IMF and government bureaucrats are portrayed as conspirators on a grand scale and, as usual, a "threat to national security". As the unrest spread, security forces opened fire, killing at least 60 people (as many as 120 according to some reports). A state of emergency and a curfew were declared on 3 January 1985, and public gatherings of more than three persons were forbidden.

As Tunisia returned to relative normality, Morocco was experiencing its own wave of mass demonstrations and street violence. In Morocco, as in Tunisia, the demonstrations were triggered by official proposals to raise the price of basic commodities, including food. As usual, the IMF put forward a major programme of "economic stabilisation", involving, among other measures, the withdrawal of subsidies on basic goods. As social unrest spread, it was countered by heavy concentrations of state security forces. At least 100 were killed (as many as 400 according to some sources) and many more injured and arrested. As in Tunisia, the unrest was blamed on "agitators".

More recently, Tunisia has been in the news for the same reason, as reported by Fanack.com (2018). On 1 January 2018, the government introduced measures aimed at reducing the budget deficit, including higher service and consumption taxes. Tunisians woke up to receive a new year present, a general hike in the prices of goods and services, including some essential items (such as fruit, vegetables and fuel) and non-essential items such as phone cards and perfumes. The motivation, as expected, was IMF conditionality, linked to its $2.9 billion loan. In this case the government was required to reduce public sector salaries, improve tax collection and crack down on tax evasion (except, of course, when tax evasion is committed by predatory foreign investors).

What followed was the same story all over again. A few complaints online turned into a wave of protests in cities including the capital Tunis, Mahdia, Siliana and Kasserine. In Thala, which made headlines during the 2011 revolution, protesters set the security forces' headquarters on fire, forcing them to withdraw. On 8 January 2018, the protests claimed their first victim, who died as a result of asphyxiation by tear gas. However, a video and several pictures surfaced online of the victim being run over by a police car, fuelling more violence and protests in the city. Over 800 people were arrested, according to United Nations figures. Furthermore, several journalists were interrogated by the police while covering the protests. Still, the government reacted by defending the economic measures, describing them as "difficult but necessary to improve the economic situation". At the same time, the opposition party was blamed for the ensuing violence, and the "leftist anarchic political parties" were accused of taking advantage of citizens' demands "to incite chaos, acts of vandalism, sabotage and looting".

Although the IMF-prescribed policies were criticised and rejected by many politicians and incited nationwide protests, they are still in place because of pressure from the IMF. Since the so-called Arab Spring, the Tunisian government has taken out various loans to cover expenses, pushing up public debt from 41% of GDP in 2010 to a staggering 71% in 2018. Jihen Chandoul, co-founder of the Tunisian Economic Observatory, accused the IMF of "imposing these reforms and causing this unrest". In an online statement, the IMF responded by saying that "the fragile economic condition of Tunisia is a result of … its model of state patronage", adding that "the IMF does not advocate austerity … (but) advocates well-designed, well-implemented, socially-balanced reforms". Of course the IMF would not spell out the criteria used to determine "well-designed" higher food prices, "well-implemented" privatisation of water and electricity, and "socially-balanced" reduction in health expenditure.

Egypt

The Egyptian "bread riots" affected most major cities in Egypt during the period 18–19 January 1977. The riots started as a spontaneous uprising by hundreds of thousands of lower-class people protesting the IMF's recommended removal of state subsidies on basic foodstuffs. Rioting by those who would have been hardest hit by the cancellation of the subsidies erupted across the country, from Aswan to Alexandria. For two days, rioters attacked targets that symbolised the prosperity of the middle class and the corruption of the regime, 79 people died in the riots, 556 were injured and over 1000 people were arrested. The protests came to an end with the deployment of the army and the re-institution of subsidies.

The causes of the Egyptian riots can be traced back to 1976, when the Egyptian government sought loans to relieve the country's debt burden, but the government was criticised (by the IMF) for subsidising basic food items. In January 1977, the government went along with IMF conditionality, announcing the removal of subsidies on flour, rice and cooking oil. That was not all, as the government announced its intention to cancel state employee bonuses and pay increases.

The riots had a strong impact upon the Egyptian government's subsequent willingness to enact unpopular economic policies. Following the riots, according to David Seddon, the Egyptian government was "extremely cautious of provoking popular protest and political unrest through the introduction of drastic austerity measures, and it approached the IMF proposals with care" (Seddon 1990). Although Egypt signed an extended Fund facility in 1978, the government's failure to adhere to IMF-imposed policy conditions resulted in only a small amount of funds being released.

In March 2017 bread riots erupted across Egypt as the government introduced major cutbacks to subsidies and ordered bakeries to reduce the sales of subsidised bread as part of a series of austerity measures affecting state rations. Those measures were taken to secure a $12 billion loan from the IMF. Police clashed with protesters in the working-class districts of Alexandria, Kafr El Sheikh, Minya and Asyut where demonstrators blocked roads and surrounded government offices while chanting "we want to eat".

Jordan

In April 1989, the Jordanian government implemented an IMF-sponsored economic adjustment and austerity plan. In response, riots erupted and subsequently spread across the country. Seven years later, in August 1996, the Jordanian government once again complied with IMF-prescribed policies, leading to another round of civil unrest. Ryan (1998) argues that while the two episodes appear identical in terms of government policy and public response, they differ considerably in terms of the government's reaction to the unrest. In 1989 the king scrambled to make concessions, but in the 1996 episode, he stood behind the government, offered no concessions and, to the contrary, threatened to use any means necessary to quell the disturbances.

Ryan (1998) points out that the macroeconomic indicators of Jordan in 1996 were similar to what they were in 1989, and argues that the problem was not in what the aggregate economic indicators say, but rather what they do not say. For example, reduction of the budget deficit was achieved by cutting back government spending, preventing public sector salaries from keeping up with inflation, and reducing the number of available public sector jobs. A comparison between the IMF riots of 1989 and 1996 shows that although the economic plans were similar and the riots themselves were virtually identical, the state's reactions were considerably different.

Jordan has been in the news recently for the same reason. Morrison (2018) suggests that Jordan could find itself becoming the next Syria if the government does not learn from previous riots and insists on cutting bread subsidies as recommended by the IMF. He predicts that this action would likely lead to protests and perhaps even popular revolt, suggesting that other solutions to the country's economic problems are available. For example, he points out that instead of cutting bread subsidies, the government should raise the sales tax and tax goods that are currently not taxed at all. This move would bring in more revenue for the government, without the risk of social revolt.

Taha (2018) deals with the same topic, describing how some 3000 people faced down a heavy security presence to gather near the prime minister's office in Amman. Hundreds responding to a call by trade unions flooded the streets of Amman and other cities to demand the fall of the government. He quotes one protester as saying that "women have started looking in rubbish bins to find food for their children, and every day we're hit by price hikes and new taxes". The IMF, on the other hand, declared that the objective was to reduce Jordan's public debt from 94% to 77% of GDP by 2021, through "reforms to bolster economic growth and gradual fiscal consolidation".

Sudan

In mid-January 2018, protests broke out across Sudan as thousands of people took to the streets to defy the government's decision to abolish subsidies on basic food items, such as bread and sugar, as well as electricity. The encounter was violent as the security forces used tear gas and live ammunition, leading to death and injuries. The government shut down several newspapers that had been active in covering the protests and numerous arrests were made.

Sudan has been weakened by the 2011 partition of the country, which was encouraged by the "west" and resulted in the loss of South Sudan where three-quarters of the country's oil reserves lie. The public budget was further hampered by the loss of oil revenue, years of US sanctions and costly wars in Darfur and in South Sudan. In November 2017, the IMF released a report based on its study team's visit to Khartoum in September, recommending the removal of bread and fuel subsidies as well as the devaluation the Sudanese pound. In December, the Sudanese National Assembly passed a budget that contained cuts in subsidies and announced the devaluation of the Sudanese pound subsequently. Both the removal of subsidies and devaluation led to a significant rise in the cost of living, thus triggering unrest.

4.5   Concluding Remarks

Food riots may occur for a variety of reasons, one of which is IMF-recommended policies requiring the removal of subsidies, perhaps leading to changes in production patterns. We cannot blame the IMF for food shortage caused by harvest failure, but we can certainly blame it for food riots caused by policies designed to achieve unnecessary ends or ends that can be achieved by other less painful means. The attitude of the IMF towards the poor in the countries subject to its conditionality provisions is at best one of total indifference. It brings to mind the story when Marie Antoinette was told that the people could not find bread, and she responded as follows: "let them eat cake".

Patel and McMichael (2009) present a detailed account of food riots. They occurred in the seventeenth century (such as the Moscow uprising of 1648), eighteenth century (such as the Boston bread riot between 1710 and 1713 and the flour war of 1775 in France), the nineteenth century (such as the flour riot of 1837 in New York City), the twentieth century (such as the meat riots that occurred in the Chilean capital, Santiago, in October 1905) and the twenty-first century (such as the 2007 West Bengal food riots). These riots were not caused by the IMF, but the number of riots caused by the IMF is substantial. In this chapter we briefly described some of those riots.

The riots and protests are initiated by the poor because they are the victims of IMF policies. While the policies are portrayed as being good for the poor—because they have positive effects on growth, employment, productivity and social welfare—they are designed to benefit predatory foreign investors, multinationals and the local oligarchs. In Table 4.1, we display some cynical interpretations of IMF recommendations. These recommendations invariably lead to riots and civil unrest as shown in Fig. 4.1.

Table 4.1   The meaning of IMF-prescribed policies

Policy	True meaning
Labour reform	Giving multinationals and oligarchs the ability to hire and fire as they wish
Fiscal reform	Cutting social expenditure while leaving military expenditure intact
Structural reform	Providing better environment for predatory foreign investors
Social security reform	Abolishing unemployment benefits and pensions
Deregulation	Removing any restrictions that may be a nuisance for predatory foreign investors
Privatisation	Surrendering public assets to predatory foreign investors
Downsizing the public sector	Firing government employees without compensation
Opening the economy	Allowing multinationals free access to domestic markets without any restrictions
Allowing a far greater role for foreign investors	Giving foreign investors the opportunity to buy high-quality public assets at fire-sale prices
Wage restraint	Freezing nominal wages, leading to falling real wages
Removal of subsidies	Making food and other essential items more expensive for the poor
Macroeconomic reform	Adopting "western"-style market-oriented macroeconomic policies
Civil service reform	Firing government employees
Transition to a private-led economy	Selling public assets to oligarchs and predatory foreign investors
Adopting prudent monetary policy	Starving productive sectors of credit and abolishing subsidised credit
Trade liberalisation	Opening up for multinationals
Attracting foreign investment	Giving concessions to foreign investors and allowing them to operate above the law
Tackling rigidities in the labour market	Allowing multinationals to hire and fire as they please, depriving workers of any rights
Enhancing efficiency	Cutting corners irrespective of environmental and other considerations
Reducing the minimum wage	Allowing multinationals to pay workers one dollar a day in wages

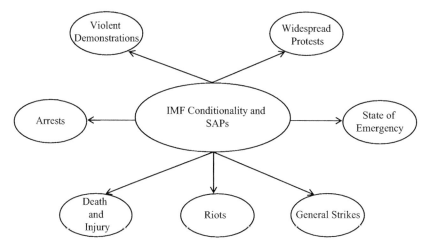

Fig. 4.1 The cause and effect

REFERENCES

Bellemare, M. F. (2014). Rising Food Prices, Food Price Volatility, and Social Unrest. http://marcfbellemare.com/wordpress/wp-content/uploads/2014/03/BellemareAJAEFoodRiotsManuscript.pdf

Brinkman, H. J., & Hendrix, C. S. (2011). Food Insecurity and Violent Conflict: Causes, Consequences, and Addressing the Challenges. World Food Programme, Occasional Papers, No. 24.

Fanack.com. (2018). Social Unrest in Tunisia: When the Expected Becomes Unexpected. https://fanack.com/tunisia/history-past-to-present/social-unrest-in-tunisia/

Marshall, A. G. (2014, July 26). IMF, World Bank, Giant Consultants Admit the Storm is Coming. World of Resistance Report. https://truthout.org/articles/world-of-resistance-report-imf-world-bank-giant-consultants-admit-the-storm-is-coming/

Morrison, N. (2018, January 9). Cutting Bread Subsidies Could Make Jordan the Next Syria. https://www.alaraby.co.uk/english/blog/2018/1/9/cutting-bread-subsidies-could-make-jordan-the-next-syria

Oxfam. (2002). Death on the Doorstep of the Summit. Oxfam Briefing Papers, No. 29.

Palast, G. (2001, April 29). IMF's Four Steps to Damnation. *The Guardian*. https://www.theguardian.com/business/2001/apr/29/business.mbas

Patel, R., & McMichael, P. (2009). A Political Economy of the Food Riot. *Review: A Journal of Fernand Braudel Center, 32*, 9–35.

Ponticelli, J., & Voth, H. J. (2017). Austerity and Anarchy: Budget Cuts and Social Unrest in Europe, 1919–2008. https://doi.org/10.2139/ssrn.1899287

Ryan, C. R. (1998). Peace, Bread and Riots: Jordan and the International Monetary Fund. *Middle East Policy, 6*, 54–66.

Seddon, D. (1986). Riot and Rebellion: Political Responses to Economic Crisis in North Africa, Tunisia, Morocco and Sudan. http://la.utexas.edu/users/hcleaver/357L/357LSeddontable.pdf

Seddon, D. (1990). The Politics of Adjustment: Egypt and the IMF, 1987–1990. *Review of African Political Economy, 47*, 95–104.

Taha, K. (2018, June 4). Jordan Senate Meets as Protests Escalate over IMF-Backed Austerity Proposed Tax Rises and Price Hikes Bring Thousands to Streets as Government Seeks 'Comprehensive National Dialogue'. https://www.timesofisrael.com/jordan-senate-meets-as-protests-escalate-over-imf-backed-austerity/

The Guardian. (2018, August 29). Argentina Seeks Emergency Release of $50bn in IMF Funds Amid Financial Crisis.

Woodroffe, J., & Ellis-Jones, M. (2000). States of Unrest: Resistance to IMF Policies in Poor Countries. *World Development Movement Report*. http://www.wdm.org.uk/cambriefs/DEBT/unrest.htm

CHAPTER 5

The Effects of IMF Operations on Social Expenditure

5.1 Introduction

Social expenditure is defined by Clements et al. (2013) simply as "public spending on education and health", although it is reasonable to think that it also covers expenditure on child care and similar items. On the other hand, Wojnilower (2017) dismisses the availability of a standard definition of social protection or of broader/overlapping terms such as "social security", "social spending/expenditure" and "social safeguards" in or outside the IMF. Accordingly, he argues that "this has sometimes resulted in the IMF and its critics seeming to talk past each other". For the purpose of this discussion, we adopt the definition used by Clements et al. (2013) that social expenditure refers to spending on health and education.

The widespread belief that IMF operations have a negative effect on social expenditure can be justified by the very nature of IMF operations and the ideology that drives it. Wojnilower (2017) presents a summary of the criticism directed at the IMF for promoting policies that weaken social protection by academics, civil society organisations and international organisations. We have to bear in mind here that what we are concerned with eventually is the ability of ordinary people to access healthcare and education, which can be affected adversely by three factors: (i) direct reduction in public social spending; (ii) poverty and inequality, which affect the ability of people to access private healthcare and education and their ability to meet out-of-pocket payments; and (iii) the mix of health

© The Author(s) 2019

I. A. Moosa, N. Moosa, *Eliminating the IMF*,
https://doi.org/10.1007/978-3-030-05761-9_5

and education providers between public and private. IMF operations have implications for all of these aspects of access to healthcare and education.

To start with, the Washington Consensus principles are not conducive to increasing social expenditure. The first commandment of fiscal policy discipline, the second commandment of redirecting public spending and the eighth commandment of the privatisation of public enterprises should have negative effects on social expenditure. IMF operations are intended for one thing and one thing only, which is to enhance the ability of borrowing countries to pay their debt to the IMF and other creditors. Anything that can be saved by cutting social expenditure is always useful for this purpose. The privatisation of healthcare and education means that they become within the reach of only the rich and privileged.

The IMF recommends policies that typically affect public expenditure on health and education as well as access and affordability, with the privatisation of public enterprises as having a profound negative effect. The Fund recommends currency devaluation, which makes imported medical equipment and medicines more expensive. The IMF prescribes austerity, which means reduction in public expenditure in general and increasing poverty with diminished ability of people to meet out-of-pocket medical expenses. The Fund recommends restructuring of foreign debt, which may involve debt-equity swap, ending with foreign investors owning healthcare facilities. It recommends free-market pricing, putting health and education beyond the affordability of ordinary people. It recommends the enhancement of the "rights" of foreign investors vis-à-vis national law, which undermines the ability of locals to access the health and education facilities run by predatory foreign investors who operate above local law. It recommends financialisation, which boosts inequality, affects adversely employment in the productive sectors of the economy and inflicts brain drain on other sectors of the economy. Eventually the supply of healthcare and education declines while prices rise, making it difficult for people to access healthcare, depriving them of what may be considered a human right. Recall the 2009 study of *The Lancet* that shows millions of deaths resulting from the shock therapy prescriptions used in Russia and former communist countries on the recommendation of the IMF (*Medical Express* 2009).

We start by presenting the view of the IMF as reflected in the writings and statements of the IMF staff. Then we explore the opposing views coming from outsiders with various beliefs and ideologies. The opposing views are then presented in a debate-like style. This is followed by a consideration of the empirical evidence and how it can be used to support two diametrically opposite views. We close with some concluding remarks.

5.2   THE VIEW OF THE IMF

The view of the IMF on the effect of its operations on social expenditure is spelled out in an in-house interview (published on the IMF's website) with Sanjeev Gupta, Deputy Director of the IMF's Fiscal Affairs Department, and Catherine Pattillo, Advisor in the Strategy, Policy and Review Department. Gupta was asked if governments with IMF-supported programmes are pressed to reduce social spending to meet agreed economic targets. His answer was in the negative as Gupta claimed that "during the global food and fuel and financial crises, IMF-supported programs have been very flexible by accommodating larger fiscal deficits and higher inflation, and by continuing to protect priority social expenditures". The IMF, according to Gupta, places "considerable emphasis on strengthening social protection for the most vulnerable", with the objective of "preserving and in most cases increasing social spending" and "protecting the most vulnerable". He attributes the constraints on health expenditure to "administrative capacity constraints, rather than excessively tight macroeconomic policies". This means that money is available but it cannot be spent effectively because of "poor national coordination", "shortcomings in the health care system" and "absorptive capacity". This sounds like confusing the cause with the effect and like blaming the victim for the mishap.

In her turn, Pattillo responded in the negative to the question if IMF-supported programmes require countries to cut social spending so that inflation can be contained because "even in those countries that had to tighten fiscal policy, social spending has been protected". Gupta rejects the view that social spending in general, and health spending in particular, has declined in countries with IMF-supported programmes, describing the claim as "untrue" by referring to evidence produced by the IMF's Independent Evaluation Office. He also refers to a 2007 study by the Center for Global Development (CGD), which reveals that the average increase in health spending as a share of GDP was larger for countries with Fund-supported programmes than in low-income countries without such programmes. This, however, is not the truth, the whole truth and nothing but the truth, as documented in the CGD study—it is convenient cherry picking.

Pattillo rejects the claim that IMF-supported programmes are associated with higher tuberculosis mortality in post-communist countries (as revealed by *The Lancet*) as "an old and baseless criticism". She argues that this claim is based on an assessment with serious methodological flaws represented by failure to control for the highly persistent nature of tuberculosis, which further biases the results. She refers to the results produced by the IMF's Research Department for the same sample of countries revealing a "small, statistically weak negative correlation between program participation and tuberculosis mortality". Naturally, the Research Department of the IMF is unlikely to publish results that indicate otherwise. Empirical work invariably allows the researcher to torture the data until the "right" results are obtained.

Gupta goes on the offensive by arguing that "IMF-supported programs play an important role in mobilizing donor support around country-owned poverty reduction strategies" and that "the IMF supports macroeconomic stability because it is a necessary condition for economic growth and poverty reduction, without which lasting improvements in public health conditions cannot be made". In response to the question if aid intended for the health sector is diverted to repay domestic debt or boost reserves, he replies by saying that "IMF-supported programs play an important role in mobilizing donor support around country-owned poverty reduction strategies" and blaming the "lack of capacity" on the ability of countries to spend on health (e.g., it takes time to hire new doctors and nurses and construct health centres).

An issue that keeps resurfacing is that IMF programmes include public sector wage-bill ceilings, which may directly or indirectly prevent desirable increases in health spending. When asked about this issue, Gupta declared that "IMF program conditionality has never included any wage-bill ceilings or hiring freezes for that matter, specifically on the health sector". He went on to say that "ceilings can be used only in exceptional circumstances where they are crucial for macroeconomic stability, and should be of limited duration, periodically reassessed, and sufficiently flexible to accommodate spending of scaled-up aid in priority social sectors". If a government is told (by the IMF) to cut public expenditure (or else), the first target is typically the wage bill. It is not necessary for the Fund to order explicitly a wage-bill ceiling, as a general expenditure ceiling would suffice.

In a recent IMF blog, Gupta and Shang (2017) reiterate the IMF declared attitude towards social spending, arguing that "over the past few decades, protecting social programs and spending on health has been a cornerstone of the IMF's support for countries". They cite a number of studies reaching the conclusion that IMF support for countries' "reforms", on average, either preserve or boost public health spending. The rationale is that without "reform", a country's economy could collapse, along with its public healthcare system. While they admit that the IMF operations may impede spending on public health in more than one way, this effect is offset by "other important factors through which the IMF's support for a country positively affects public health spending". The underlying idea, it seems, is that if a country reduces social spending for the sake of macro-economic stability, higher growth in the long run will provide resources for health and education. Those who put forward this proposition seem to overlook what J.M. Keynes said at one time—that in the long run we are all dead (Keynes 1923).

Gupta and Shang (2017) suggest several ways whereby the IMF pro-vides support for social spending, including the following: (i) the eco-nomic and financial stability promoted by IMF-prescribed policies can help governments raise revenue to finance healthcare; (ii) IMF support is conducive to receiving more financing from other donors, which boosts the resources available to finance priority spending on health and other social programmes; (iii) IMF-prescribed tax reform boosts government revenue; and (iv) improving the overall efficiency of spending can help governments finance spending on health and education. They also men-tion "other ways the IMF can help a country in a crisis with health spend-ing", referring in particular to the experience of the countries affected by the Ebola epidemic (Guinea, Liberia and Sierra Leone) and claiming a positive influence of IMF financial support. So, it is all about convincing people not to worry about the present as things will be brighter as long as the IMF is in charge. This is like saying that poor people should not worry about poverty as they will all realise the "American dream" and become billionaires eventually.

The IMF website contains a large number of items on the Ebola crisis, including press releases, country reports, IMF surveys, podcasts and state-ments (http://www.imf.org/external/np/fad/ebola/). This is what the Fund says about the Ebola outbreak:

> The involvement of the IMF reflects the mounting macroeconomic impact of the crisis on countries that were making strides in overcoming years of fragility and instability. The additional financial assistance to help combat the epidemic fits within the Fund's mandate to support its member countries in times of economic and social stress with balance of payments and fiscal support.

Gupta (2014) defends the IMF with respect to its role in the Ebola crisis in response to a comment in *The Lancet* that accused the Fund of playing a role in the outbreak. He claims that it is not correct to say that healthcare expenditures declined in affected countries, claiming that these countries experienced an increase in health spending as a percentage of GDP (without saying whether the increase materialised because of or despite the role of the IMF). He also rejects as incorrect the claim that the IMF requires caps on the public sector wage bill, which is counterfactual. Gupta puts the blame squarely on civil wars and pressure on already fragile infrastructure and healthcare systems. While this is true, IMF-prescribed policies aggravated the situation.

In a blog, Clements and Gupta (2017) reiterate their defence of the IMF, their employer, arguing against the proposition that "the programs the IMF supports in low-income countries hurt the most vulnerable by forcing cuts in social spending", describing it as a "misconception". They make the following claims: (i) social spending increased at a faster pace in countries with programmes compared to those without and (ii) the benefits for social spending have accelerated over time in low-income countries. While they admit that IMF-supported programmes are not the only determinants of a country's social spending, they suggest that some statistical techniques can "distil the impact of an IMF-supported program, as distinct from these other factors". Again, they reiterate the "numerous channels through which programmes help spur higher spending in education and health", which include (i) reforms that boost government revenues and economic growth, (ii) mobilisation of donor financing and (iii) debt relief. Their boss, Christine Lagarde, shares the sentiment by referring to the "IMF's strong commitment to protect health and education spending and the most vulnerable during challenging economic reforms". She adds:

> Safeguarding social spending is critical because women, young people, seniors, and the poor often lack the political leverage to promote their economic well-being. By protecting the health and skills of vulnerable groups, growth will be stronger, more durable, and more inclusive.

Lagarde (2017) goes on about further steps to be taken by the IMF, including the following: (i) defining programme targets more explicitly, (ii) improving the design of social safety nets and (iii) delivering better outcomes by stepping up collaboration with governments and development partners.

5.3   The Opposing Views

In its mild (and diplomatic) criticism of the IMF, the Center for Global Development (2007) suggests that "the IMF has not done enough to explore a full range of fiscal policy options, including more ambitious but still feasible paths for higher government spending, including on health", suggesting that the IMF is in favour of domestic debt reduction or external reserve increases over additional spending even when macroeconomic conditions are quite favourable. It is also argued that "wage bill ceilings have been overused in IMF programs, especially in Africa". The CGD report suggests that although IMF programmes have not imposed ceilings on wages or hiring in health (or education), attempts by the IMF to accommodate hiring for these sectors within aggregate wage-bill ceilings have failed.

To remedy the situation, the Center makes several recommendations: (i) the IMF should help countries explore a broader range of feasible options for the fiscal deficit and public spending; (ii) the Fund should adopt and make public clearer guidelines on what is expected of IMF staff in analysing the consequences of alternative aid paths and on what should drive IMF signals about aid levels; (iii) the IMF should do more to promote fuller and more timely information about expectations for aid in its programmes; (iv) wage-bill ceilings should be dropped from IMF programmes except in cases where a loss of budgetary control over payrolls threatens macroeconomic stability; (v) IMF programmes should give greater emphasis to short-term expenditure smoothing, particularly when macroeconomic instability is no longer a significant threat; and (vi) the Fund should be more transparent and proactive in discussing the rationale for its policy advice and the assumptions underlying its programmes.

The IMF claims that it has helped put an end to the Ebola crisis, but this view is not shared by external observers. *The Lancet* (2015) argues that the IMF might have contributed to the circumstances that enabled the crisis to arise in the first place and that a major reason why the outbreak spread so rapidly was the weakness of health systems in the region. The *Lancet* comment refers to conditionalities that "require recipient governments to adopt policies that have been criticised for prioritising short-term economic objectives over investment in health and education". The so-called economic reform programmes in the region exposed to the Ebola outbreak required the following: (i) reductions in government spending, prioritisation of debt service and bolstering of foreign exchange reserves; (ii) caps on the public sector wage bill and hence on the funds needed to hire and remunerate doctors, nurses and other healthcare professionals; and (iii) decentralisation of healthcare systems, which made it difficult to mobilise co-ordinated, central responses to disease outbreaks (see, e.g., Homedes and Ugalde 2005; Djibuti et al. 2007).

Writing in *The Guardian*, Kentikelenis et al. (2016a) accuse the IMF of not living up to its own hype on social protection. While the IMF claims that it helps governments to protect and even boost social spending, this claim, according to them, is "unfounded". They argue on the following lines:

> Stringent IMF-mandated austerity measures explain part of this trend. As countries engaged in excessive fiscal belt-tightening to meet the IMF's macroeconomic targets, few funds were left for maintaining social spending at adequate levels. These shortfalls suggest that social spending targets are accorded—at best—secondary importance in IMF programmes, and that the organisation has not lived up to its own hype of promoting social protection.

For example, Guinea (one of the affected countries) has received financial support from the IMF to improve economic conditions, while allowing for increased investment in social policies, but when the IMF-prescribed fiscal austerity was observed, the country failed to meet social spending targets. In 2014, the Guinean authorities wrote to the IMF to say the following: "unfortunately, because of the reduction in spending, including on domestic investment, it was not possible to respect the … targets for spending in priority sectors". Kentikelenis et al. (2016b) make it explicit that "under direct IMF tutelage, some of the poorest countries underfunded their social protection systems" and recommend that the IMF can and must adapt its practices. In doing so, they suggest, the Fund can learn from others by scaling up existing collaboration with the International Labour Organization, a leader in universal social protection.

Stubbs and Kentikelenis (2017) suggest that while the IMF provides financial assistance to countries in economic trouble, its policy proposals do not always yield positive results for the countries it purports to help. In West Africa, they argue, the IMF has exerted a unique influence on the evolution of health systems in a number of countries with a combined population of more than 330 million, including Benin, Burkina Faso, Côte d'Ivoire, Gambia, Ghana, Guinea-Bissau, Liberia, Mali, Niger,

Nigeria, Senegal, Sierra Leone and Togo. While West African health systems were weak before the IMF got involved, thanks to legacies of conflict and weak state capacity, they suggest that "reforms demanded by the IMF over the past two decades in exchange for loans have undermined the ability of national governments to repair their historical problems". The IMF, according to them, is "responsible for designing inappropriate or dogmatic policies that undermine the development of health systems". They explain the role of the IMF in influencing health policy in West Africa by arguing that the Fund is a "tool of the Western economic powers, primarily the US and Europe" and that "the former imperial powers continue to use the IMF to promote a neoliberal agenda across the world". They make the interesting observation that the IMF, which is headquartered in Washington, DC, is "largely staffed with Anglo-Saxon economists who are tasked with leading responses to unfamiliar environments in faraway places".

In October 2017, the Global Coalition for Social Protection Floors (2017) wrote to the IMF to suggest that "the IMF's approach towards social protection has been principally oriented around the desire to reduce social protection coverage and contain expenditure, rather than ensuring adequate levels of protection for all". By reducing coverage, they meant targeting social protection spending towards sub-groups of the population. Ortiz et al. (2015) list many reasons why targeting is not the best approach, particularly in developing countries where a large proportion of the population are living in poverty. These include adding to costs and administrative burden and creating two-tier systems, in addition to leading to under-coverage, meaning that many of the most vulnerable may be excluded. Griffiths and Brunswijck (2018) argue that "despite this major failing of targeted approaches, the IMF keeps pushing targeted social programmes through its loan conditionality and policy advice".

5.4   THE DEBATE

The IMF proposes three channels through which its programmes are linked to strengthening of health systems. The first is that IMF-prescribed policies enhance economic growth and raise tax revenues, thereby allowing governments to invest in public health (Clements et al. 2013; Crivelli and Gupta 2016). The second is that social spending floors shelter sensitive expenditures from austerity measures (Gupta et al. 2000; Gupta 2010; IMF 2015). The third channel is that the implementation of the IMF's policy advice is conducive to foreign aid and investment (Clements et al. 2013; IEO 2007). In contrast, the critics contend that adequate investment in health is hampered by pressure to meet rigid fiscal deficit targets and by diverting funds away from the health sector to repay debt or boost reserves (Kentikelenis 2015; Kentikelenis et al. 2015a, b, 2016a, b; Ooms and Schrecker 2005; Stuckler and Basu 2009; Stuckler et al. 2008, 2011). If, as the evidence indicates, IMF-prescribed policies depress economic growth, the resources available to fund healthcare shrink (Barro and Lee 2005; Dreher 2006; Przeworski and Vreeland 2000). Furthermore, these policies are not conducive to the attraction of health aid (Stubbs et al. 2016). Jensen (2004) demonstrates that countries having IMF agreements, ceteris paribus, attract 25% less FDI inflows than countries not under IMF agreements, a result that should be valid for development aid.

IMF policies have both direct and indirect consequences for health expenditure, which can be construed to be positive and negative, depending on who is expressing the underlying view. The first of the positive direct effects, as mentioned earlier, is that the IMF operations are subject to conditions designed to protect social expenditure from the adverse consequences of adjustment policies (Gupta et al. 2000). Kentikelenis et al. (2015b) disagree, arguing that spending targets are often expressed as shares of GDP, and since the IMF policies cause economic contraction, total expenditure declines. Furthermore, the extent to which these conditions are implemented and the importance that the Fund attaches to monitoring them have been questioned (Kentikelenis et al. 2014; Goldsborough 2007; Oxfam 1995).

It is also claimed that IMF policies often go beyond spending conditionality to foster a more active reshaping of the health sector, including the enhancement of the role played by the private sector in healthcare provision (Benson 2001; Gupta et al. 2000; Loewenson 1995; Turshen 1999), the introduction of cost-sharing for the use of health services (IEO 2003; Pitt 1993; Sen and Koivusalo 1998) and decentralising health services (Kentikelenis et al. 2014). Kentikelenis et al. (2015b) argue that while it is possible that the revenue generated from patients or hospital privatisation may be reinvested in the health system (thus raising spending), the proceeds may be diverted to other areas of spending. The enhancement of the role of the private sector can hardly be a substitute for public health expenditure as private healthcare is beyond the means of the vast majority of people, particularly in low-income countries. Even in rich countries such as the US, people die either because they do not have private health coverage or because they are denied a specific form of treatment for one reason or another. This is probably the reason why we often hear the terms "medical refugees" and "dental refugees" in reference to Americans seeking treatment in Mexico. The same criticism applies to the introduction of cost-sharing for the use of health services and the decentralisation of health services.

What is not clear here is how the proceeds of the privatisation of public hospitals are invested in the "health system", given that privatisation means putting an end to public healthcare. It could be that reinvesting the privatisation proceeds in the health system means subsidising private hospitals owned and operated by oligarchs and predatory foreign entrepreneurs. This means that ordinary people are deprived from free or cheap public healthcare and face the eventuality of paying $5000 a night for a private hospital bed—the good news being that the bed would cost only $4000 a night because of the subsidies. It is either that this is a bargain not to be missed or that common sense no longer has a place.

Furthermore, it is claimed (on behalf of the IMF) that public health expenditure is subject to the "resource effect" arising from the low interest credit provided under its programmes. The additional resources, as the argument goes, could be used to boost expenditure to meet health priorities. However, it is unlikely that this effect will materialise because the extra resources will be used to repay external debt (Gould 2003). In addition, it is argued (on behalf of the Fund) that the IMF operations give the underlying country a "stamp of approval", which boosts aid flows (Clements et al. 2013). While there is some evidence for the link between foreign aid and Fund programmes (Bird and Rowlands 2007), it is not necessarily the case that those funds will be directed to health (Rowden 2009b; Stuckler et al. 2011) or that they will be channelled through the government (Lu et al. 2010; Sridhar and Woods 2010).

While the IMF always claims that its programmes strengthen health systems (Clements et al. 2013; Gupta 2010, 2015), it has long been criticised for impeding the development of public health systems (Baker 2010; Benson 2001; Goldsborough 2007; Kentikelenis et al. 2015a, b; 2016a, b; Stuckler and Basu 2009; Stuckler et al. 2008, 2011). A qualitative analysis of IMF programmes in Guinea, Liberia and Sierra Leone found that the IMF contributed to the failure of health systems to develop, thereby exacerbating the Ebola crisis (Kentikelenis et al. 2015a). The recent experience shows that the IMF's policy advice is associated with diminishing public health resources, difficulties in hiring and retaining health workers, and unsuccessful health sector reforms. Van der Hoeven and Stewart (1993) suggest that "neither the IMF nor the World Bank recognized the need to take any special actions to protect the poor".

In a previous section we outlined the interview with Sanjeev Gupta and Catherine Pattillo, in which die-hard arguments were put forward in defence of their employer, the IMF. In response to this interview, Rowden (2009a) raises several points as to why the IMF is likely to reduce spending on health, which triggered a response and a response to the response. In particular he asserts that "the IMF is not a development organization per se, but acts to ensure that sovereign debt payments are made on time to external lenders and that creditworthiness is maintained", which means that "its short-term priority for borrowers is to generate increased exports and earn foreign exchange which may be used to repay creditors". He suggests that "by looking to the IMF for its assessment of the adequacy or 'soundness' of a recipient country's macroeconomic policies before giving out foreign aid each year, bilateral and multilateral aid donors have wrongly afforded tremendous leverage and power to the IMF". The "soundness" of macroeconomic policy typically means keeping inflation in check, which is inconsistent with currency devaluation that leads to imported inflation.

The IMF is an ideologically-driven organisation, adopting the neoliberal ideas of laissez-faire and the Washington Consensus. Rowden (2009a) refers to the IMF's "ideological disposition that prioritizes short-term financial sector variables in macroeconomic policy to the subordination or neglect of real sector variables, such as long-term developmental goals, industrialization, higher employment or increased public investment", arguing that "such a position is associated with the school of monetarism within neoclassical economics". Policies that induce a long-term trend of low growth, low employment and low public investment are associated with chronically insufficient health budgets and dilapidated health infrastructure.

Typically IMF-imposed macroeconomic targets include an annual inflation rate in the range of 5–7% and a budget deficit below 3% of GDP. The restrictiveness of these policies, according to Rowden (2009a), "undermines the ability of domestic industries to generate higher levels of productive capacity, employment, and GDP output—and thus, tax revenues—than otherwise could be the case under more expansionary fiscal and monetary policy options". As a result, the government is deprived of higher levels of tax revenue for recurrent expenditures and for long-term public investment as a percentage of GDP. A report published by the

Government Accountability Office (2001) on IMF loans suggests that "policies that are overly concerned with macroeconomic stability may turn out to be too austere, lowering economic growth from its optimal level and impeding progress on poverty reduction". Likewise, Pollin and Zhu (2006) contend that "there is no justification for inflation-targeting policies as they are currently being practiced throughout the middle- and low-income countries". The Center for Global Development (2007) found that "the empirical evidence does not justify pushing inflation to these levels in low-income countries".

On 14 November 2007, the House Financial Services Committee of the U.S. Congress sent a letter to the Managing Director of the IMF, expressing concern about "the IMF's adherence to overly-rigid macroeconomic targets", suggesting that "it is particularly troubling to us that the IMF's policy positions do not reflect any consensus view among economists on appropriate inflation targets" (Financial Services Committee 2007). It is true that high inflation can be damaging for investment and growth, but how high is high? Controlling inflation should be looked upon in terms of costs and benefits. Rowden (2009a) refers to the "empirically unjustifiable tight fiscal and monetary targets in non-transparent meetings with central bank and finance officials behind closed doors".

In a reply to Rowden (2009a), Gupta and Pattillo identify three principal criticisms that require a response: (i) IMF policies keep budget deficit targets below 3% of GDP; (ii) the IMF has very little empirical evidence to justify pushing inflation down to the 5–7% level; and (iii) the IMF's policies for borrowing countries are primarily designed for achieving short-term priorities, which could be in conflict with successful long-term economic development strategies or health goals. They respond to the first point by citing some IMF reports claiming that "the evidence does not support the view that IMF-supported programs adopt a one-size-fits-all approach to fiscal adjustment" and that "there was no evidence that IMF-supported programs were overly tight". As far as point (ii) is concerned, they pick selective evidence to claim that 5% is the beginning of the inflation-related death zone, without mentioning what costs are involved. For point (iii) they claim that the statement is false because "Fund-supported programs are framed in the context of a medium-term macroeconomic framework that incorporates long-term development objectives". Ironically they claim that "the objective of IMF-supported programs is to promote high and sustained growth, which will improve the well-being of the poor and create fiscal space for increasing priority spending, including on health". Tell that to the people of dozens of countries that have experienced IMF-ignited riots and civil unrest with all of the "trimmings" that came with them.

Rowden (2009a) replies by referring to biased sampling and suggests that the results would be different if the sample went back to 1980. Furthermore, he suggests that Gupta and Pattillo do not address a central concern—the fall in public investment as a percentage of GDP. Nor do they explain how and under what conditions the targets may be raised. Furthermore, Rowden notes that Gupta and Pattillo do not address the concerns raised in a number of studies, including those of the Government Accountability Office (2001), Pollin and Zhu (2006), the Center for Global Development (2007), and the letter to the IMF from the Financial Services Committee (2007).

Another exchange was initiated by Stuckler et al. (2011), who suggest that "IMF macro-economic policies, which specifically advise governments to divert aid to reserves to cope with aid volatility and keep government spending low, could be causing the displacement of health aid". They attempt to find out whether aid displacement was greater when countries accepted loans from the IMF between 1996 and 2006 and conclude that "health system spending grew at about half the speed when countries were exposed to the IMF than when they were not". Glassman (2011) comes to the rescue of the IMF by describing as a "controversial conclusion" (of Stuckler et al.) that IMF policies could be causing the displacement of health aid and showing her dislike of the fact that this article was picked up by *The Guardian* (2011). In particular, she argues on the basis of econometric grounds by suggesting that "the paper fails to document the econometric strategy used to reach their conclusion" and that "comparisons of health spending in countries with and without programs are subject to statistical biases in different directions, which are again influenced by the same factors that affected a country's decision to enter an IMF-supported program in the first place".

In a comment on Glassman's defence of the IMF, Rowden attributes the observation that various studies have inconsistently found differences or no difference between IMF programme and non-IMF programme countries to "the ideological biases that underpin them", arguing that "many current finance ministry and central bank officials who have gone to school in the last 20–30 years have largely been taught one thing—and one thing only—that the only 'prudent' and 'sound' option for fiscal and monetary policies is the very conservative one favoured by the Reagan and

Thatcher governments steeped in the school of monetarism within neo-classical economics". According to this line of thinking, all other viable options have subsequently been dismissed as "imprudent" and "unsound". Rowden concludes that "it should not matter if a country has an IMF program or not, as its fiscal and monetary policies are likely subject to the same sharp right-wing turn taken in the economics profession 30 years ago, from which it has yet to recover". This means that IMF-like policies may be implemented, on ideological grounds, without the IMF demanding that.

In another comment on Glassman's piece, a commentator (who was unimpressed by Glassman lecturing everyone on the difference between causation and correlation) likens the IMF's role of a lender of last resort to the behaviour of colonial powers in the seventeenth–nineteenth centuries. During that period, whenever a country in Latin America, the Middle East, North Africa or Southeast Asia defaulted on its debt, the creditors (almost always the British, French or Dutch) would typically invade the country, take over their public finances and devote them to paying down the debt, regardless of the consequences for public health (and for everything else, for that matter). When or if the debt was paid off, the creditors would set up either a permanent colonial administration or a loyal, dependent client state.

5.5   The Empirical Evidence

Debates over controversial economic issues typically involve the presentation of empirical evidence supporting opposing views. The empirical evidence is derived by constructing and estimating models used to test hypotheses and generate forecasts. The problem is that econometrics is a "con art" that can be used to prove almost anything, which is very dangerous when it is combined with ideology and very convenient for those seeking support for prior beliefs (Moosa 2017). These days economists with opposite views of the world do not go on a quest for the truth, but rather manipulate their models to produce results that prove the validity of their views. Take, for example, the gun debate: some have produced empirical evidence showing that more guns lead to less crime (which is music to the ears of the gun lobby), while others have shown the opposite, that more guns lead to more crime. Common sense tells us that more guns lead to more crime, and no amount of fake empirical evidence should convince us otherwise. Unfortunately, but for some conveniently, economists choose to forget about common sense and put more faith in numbers coming out of a computer. This is why they test the untestable and the obvious, and this is why controversies remain controversies.

What is true for the gun debate is also true of the empirical studies used to support opposing views on the effect of IMF operations on social expenditure. The evidence produced by the IMF staff and supporters shows that IMF operations boost social expenditure, but the evidence produced by others shows otherwise. A sample of the empirical results is displayed in Table 5.1. The controversy often involves attempts to discredit the validity of the empirical results produced by those holding the opposite or a different view.

Table 5.1   Findings of empirical studies

Study	Conclusion
Gupta et al. (1998)	Since the mid-1980s real per capita spending on education and health has increased for countries with IMF-supported adjustment programmes despite the fiscal consolidation often required by those programmes.
IEO (2003)	The presence of an IMF-supported programme does not reduce social spending—rather, it is associated with increased public spending in health and education measured as a share of GDP or total spending, or in real terms compared with a situation without a programme.
Nooruddin and Simmons (2006)	While democracies allocate larger shares of their budgets to public services in the absence of IMF programmes, the difference between democracies and non-democracies disappears under IMF programmes.
Huber et al. (2008)	A higher level of health expenditure is associated with IMF programmes and a negative association is observed with social security and welfare spending.
Clements et al. (2013)	Education and health spending has risen during IMF-supported programmes at a faster pace than in developing countries as a whole.
Kentikelenis et al. (2015b)	Fund programmes are associated with higher health expenditures only in Sub-Saharan African countries, which historically spent less than any other region. This relation is negative for other low-income countries.
Stubbs et al. (2017a)	IMF-prescribed policies reduce the potential for investment in health, put a limit on the numbers of doctors and nurses, and lead to budget execution challenges in health systems. IMF conditionality impedes progress towards the attainment of universal health coverage.
Daoud et al. (2017)	IMF programmes reduce the protective effect of parental education on child health, particularly in rural areas. IMF conditionality reduces the protective effect of parents' education on child malnourishment by no less than 17%. Similar adverse effects are observed in sanitation, shelter and healthcare access (including immunisation).

In his response to Stubbs et al. (2017a), Gupta (2017) raises several broad methodological issues: drawing causal inferences from qualitative methods, addressing endogeneity when the counterfactual is almost never observed in reality and interpreting findings from qualitative and quantitative methods. Thus he declares the following: (i) the qualitative method is based on a systematic search of document archive, and the nature of the description in these documents suggests that the findings from the qualitative methods are mostly selective and anecdotal; (ii) the qualitative methods may have failed to identify other important pathways; (iii) addressing the endogeneity problem, otherwise the wrong conclusion may be drawn; (iv) the interpretation of the findings from the quantitative analysis appears incomplete and may lead to misunderstanding; and (v) it is important for the article to cast its findings in terms of the relevant literature that has studied the impact of IMF programmes on public health spending in developing countries. He concludes that "while the proposed new methodology by the authors represents an improvement, the results derived from it are inaccurate and misleading". Stubbs et al. (2017b) reply meticulously to Gupta and conclude that structural adjustment programmes should be judged by their effects on the human condition. They argue that "in an era of global uncertainty and important challenges to international organizations, the IMF could best address criticism by reforming its practices, thereby living up to its own standards on social protection, rather than continuing to deny evidence".

Metinsoy (2016) questions the results of Clements et al. (2013), arguing that "the finding is unexpected, since earlier studies demonstrated an unequivocal relationship in the opposite direction (i.e. that IMF programmes reduce social spending)". In an attempt to resolve the contradictory conclusions in the literature, she argues that social spending increases in a specific IMF programme type, namely Poverty Reduction and Growth Facility (PRGF) programmes, which are designed for less developed countries (LDCs) and envisage an increase in targeted spending in health and education. Alternatively, the stand-by arrangements or extended Fund facility does not produce a similar impact. She calls for more qualitative studies of IMF programmes in order to shed light on their human and social effects, arguing that "broad correlations between social spending and IMF programmes may not reflect the full breadth of their effect in programme countries". Furthermore, she points out that non-PRGF programmes often do not include clauses related directly to social spending while imposing upper limits on expenditure, implying significant welfare retrenchment measures and cuts in social services by governments.

The problem with the empirical studies of the relation between health expenditure and IMF-prescribed policies is that they depend on regression equations that contain a large number of explanatory variables representing empirical models that have no corresponding theoretical models. This methodology, predominantly based on cross-sectional and panel data, produces results that are highly sensitive to the selected set of explanatory variables, model specification and variable measurement. It is this problem that prompted Edward Leamer's article "Let's Take the Con out of Econometrics" (Leamer 1983). The Leamer critique revolves around the proposition that a regression model with a large number of potential explanatory variables can be used to prove almost anything and produce results (after extensive data mining) that support prior beliefs. For example, Moosa (2012, 2017) demonstrates that the same data set can be used to show that either of the two theories of capital structure is superior to the other, simply by changing the set of explanatory variables.

It seems, therefore, that the evidence on whether the IMF-sponsored programmes have a positive or negative impact on health expenditure is mixed. However, it is quite obvious that, somehow, the studies conducted by the IMF's staff or supporters show unequivocally that the IMF has done a wonderful job in promoting health expenditure, which is counterintuitive, to say the least. These results are engineered for the purpose of self-preservation. No empirical evidence is needed to support common sense, and common sense tells us that IMF operations exert a negative effect on social spending. Common sense tells us, inter alia, that "although increased social protection spending seems to be consistently supported by the IMF, its budget-cut requirements effectively limit the fiscal space available to increase social protection and anti-crisis programs" (Rowden 2010); that "the IMF continues to prioritize macroeconomic stability over all other development and health concerns" (Baker 2010); and that "negative health consequences of IMF adjustment programs are apparent in the immediate aftermath of signing an agreement as well as years after the adoption of one of these types of loan programs" (Hoddie and Hartzell 2014). And there is more where these came from (see the collection in Wojnilower 2017).

5.6   Concluding Remarks

Metinsoy (2016) suggests a near consensus that IMF programmes are likely to reduce welfare benefits, stir opposition and cause discontent in programme countries. As a result, she argues that scholars have recently moved beyond this simple correlation and started disaggregating the programmes and their impact on separate domestic groups. The proponents of these two views (i.e., IMF operations are good or bad for health expenditure) have produced contrasting evidence. Unfortunately, empirical work in economics has been all about proving prior beliefs, which can be done with ease by playing around with model specification, variable definitions and measurement, and estimation methods. This is why a trend has recently emerged to deal with the sensitivity of the results with respect to variations in the model. However, if we combine empirical results with common sense, intuition and what happens on the ground, we will reach the conclusion that the IMF operations depress health expenditure. After all, the IMF is not a development agency—it is out there to allow multinationals to acquire public assets without paying much in the countries where it operates and to make sure that those countries pay their debt. The last thing the IMF cares about is the health and well-being of the people in those countries. After all, and as Rowden (2009b) puts it, the IMF follows the "deadly ideas of neoliberalism", thus undermining public health.

In a tweet on 22 June 2018, the IMF declared that it was "reviewing its policy on social spending (health and education, social insurance, and social assistance spending)" and invited comments. The following are some of the comments on the tweet:

- Forgive all the debt owed, turn in your corporate leadership to stand trial for corruption and crimes against humanity and dissolve yourselves, distributing all your holdings to the countries you've ruined
- Debt relief is certainly one of the approaches through which you can make health and education more accessible.
- Without free education, free healthcare, and social intervention the world is always going to drift to a bad agenda … even for the neoliberals like you. It is time for you to recognise that inequality is bad for business.

IMF operations have an adverse effect on public spending on health and education because the Fund demands spending cuts and redirection. These measures have an adverse effect on the ability of people to pay for private healthcare through austerity, poverty and the rising cost of healthcare resulting, for example, from currency devaluation and the practices of predatory private suppliers of healthcare. IMF operations cause riots and pollution, giving rise to injury and deteriorating health, which require more spending on healthcare. Through both supply and demand factors, IMF operations reduce per capita consumption of healthcare. Last, but not least, IMF operations worsen income and wealth inequality (e.g., via privatisation and financialisation), giving rise to inequality with respect to the consumption of healthcare.

REFERENCES

Baker, B. K. (2010). The Impact of the International Monetary Fund's Macroeconomic Policies on the AIDS Pandemic. *International Journal of Health Services, 40*, 347–363.

Barro, R., & Lee, J. W. (2005). IMF Programs: Who Is Chosen and What Are the Effects? *Journal of Monetary Economics, 52*, 1245–1269.

Benson, J. S. (2001). The Impact of Privatization on Access in Tanzania. *Social Science &. Medicine, 52*, 1903–1916.

Bird, G., & Rowlands, D. (2007). The IMF and the Mobilisation of Foreign Aid. *Journal of Development Studies, 43*, 856–870.

Center For Global Development. (2007). Does The IMF Constrain Health Spending in Poor Countries? Evidence and an Agenda for Action. https://www.cgdev.org/files/14103_file_IMF_report.pdf

Clements, B., & Gupta, S. (2017, December 6). When Reality Doesn't Bite—Misconceptions about the IMF and Social Spending. https://www.huffingtonpost.com/benedict-clements/when-reality-doesnt-bitem_b_943862.html

Clements, B., Gupta, S., & Nozaki, M. (2013). What Happens to Social Spending in IMF-Supported Programmes? *Applied Economics, 45*, 4022–4033.

Crivelli, E., & Gupta, S. (2016). Does Conditionality in IMF-Supported Programs Promote Revenue Reform? *International Tax Public Finance, 23*, 550.

Daoud, A., Nosrati, E., Reinsberg, B., Kentikelenis, A. E., Stubbs, T. H., & King, L. P. (2017). Impact of International Monetary Fund programs on Child Health. *PNAS, 114*, 6492–6497.

Djibuti, M., Rukhadze, N., Hotchkiss, D. R., Eisele, T. P., & Silvestre, E. A. (2007). Health Systems Barriers to Effective Use of Infectious Disease Surveillance Data in the Context of Decentralization in Georgia: A Qualitative Study. *Health Policy, 83*, 323–331.

Dreher, A. (2006). IMF and Economic Growth: The Effects of Programs, Loans, and Compliance with Conditionality. *World Development, 34*, 769–788.

Financial Services Committee. (2007, November 14). Letter to the Managing Director of the IMF from the House Financial Services Committee of the US Congress.

Glassman, A. (2011, January 19). Bring Out the Punching Bag Again: The IMF, Aid, and Public Spending on Health. *Global Health Policy Blog*. https://www.

cgdev.org/blog/bring-out-punching-bag-again-imf-aid-and-public-spending-health

Global Coalition for Social Protection Floors. (2017, October 25). Statement to the IMF on the Findings of the Evaluation Report and the IMF's Approach Towards Social Protection. http://www.socialprotectionfloorscoalition.org/2017/10/statement-to-the-imf-on-the-findings-of-the-evaluation-report-and-the-imfs-approach-towards-social-protection/

Goldsborough, D. (2007). *Does the IMF Constrain Health Spending in Poor Countries? Evidence and an Agenda for Action.* Washington, DC: Center for Global Development.

Gould, E. R. (2003). Money Talks: Supplementary Financiers and International Monetary Fund Conditionality. *International Organizations, 57*, 551–586.

Government Accountability Office. (2001). International Monetary Fund: Few Changes Evident in Design of New Lending Program for Poor Countries, Washington, DC.

Griffiths, J., & Brunswijck, G. (2018, May 15). IMF Conditionality: Still Undermining Healthcare and Social Protection?. http://www.cadtm.org/IMF-conditionality-still

Gupta, S. (2010). Response of the International Monetary Fund to its Critics. *International Journals of Health Services, 40*, 323–326.

Gupta, S. (2014, December 22). IMF Response to the Lancet Article on "The International Monetary Fund and the Ebola Outbreak". http://www.imf.org/en/News/Articles/2015/09/28/04/54/vc122214

Gupta, S. (2015). Response to "The international Monetary Fund and the Ebola Outbreak". *Lancet Global Health, 3*, 78.

Gupta, S. (2017). Can a Causal Link be Drawn? A Commentary on "The Impact of IMF Conditionality on Government Health Expenditure: A Cross-National Analysis of 16 West African Nations". *Social Science & Medicine, 181*, 199–201.

Gupta, S., & Shang, B. (2017). Public Spending on Health Care under IMF-Supported Programs. https://blogs.imf.org/2017/03/09/public-spending-on-health-care-under-imf-supported-programs/#more-17249

Gupta, S., Clements, B., & Tiongson, E. (1998). Public Spending on Human Development. *Finance and Development, 35*, 10–13.

Gupta, S., Dicks-Mireaux, L., Khemani, R., McDonald, C., & Verhoeven, M. (2000). Social Issues in IMF-Supported Programs. IMF Occasional Papers, No. 191.

Hoddie, M., & Hartzell, C. A. (2014). Short-Term Pain, Long-Term Gain? The Effects of IMF Economic Reform Programs on Public Health Performance. *Social Science Quarterly, 95*, 1042–2014.

Homedes, N., & Ugalde, A. (2005). Why Neoliberal Health Reforms Have Failed in Latin America. *Health Policy, 71*, 83–96.

Huber, E., Mustillo, T., & Stephens, J. D. (2008). Politics and Social Spending in Latin America. *Journal of Politics, 70,* 420–436.

IEO. (2003). *Fiscal Adjustment in IMF-Supported Programs.* Washington, DC: IMF Independent Evaluation Office.

IEO. (2007). *The IMF and Aid to Sub-Saharan Africa.* Washington, DC: IMF Independent Evaluation Office.

IMF. (2015). Protecting the Most Vulnerable under IMF-Supported Programs. IMF Factsheet. http://www.imf.org/external/np/exr/facts/protect.htm

Jensen, N. (2004). Crisis, Conditions, and Capital: The Effect of International Monetary Fund Agreements on Foreign Direct Investment Inflows. *Journal of Conflict Resolution, 48,* 194–210.

Kentikelenis, A. (2015). Bailouts, Austerity and the Erosion of Health Coverage in Southern Europe and Ireland. *European Journal of Public Health, 25,* 365–366.

Kentikelenis, A., King, L., McKee, M., & Stuckler, D. (2014). The International Monetary Fund and the Ebola Outbreak. *The Lancet Global Health,* 1–2. https://doi.org/10.1016/S2214-109X(14)70377-8.

Kentikelenis, A., King, L., McKee, M., & Stuckler, D. (2015a). The International Monetary Fund and the Ebola Outbreak. *Lancet Global Health, 3,* 69–70.

Kentikelenis, A., Stubbs, T., & King, L. (2015b). Structural Adjustment and Public Spending on Health: Evidence from IMF Programs in Low-Income Countries. *Social Science & Medicine, 126,* 169–176.

Kentikelenis, A., Stubbs, T., & King, L. (2016a, May 25). The IMF Has Not Lived Up to Its Own Hype on Social Protection. *The Guardian.*

Kentikelenis, A., Stubbs, T., & King, L. (2016b). IMF Conditionality and Development Policy Space, 1985–2014. *Review of International Political Economy, 23,* 543–582.

Keynes, J. M. (1923). *A Tract on Monetary Reform.* London: Macmillan.

Lagarde, C. (2017, June 6). Protecting Education and Health Spending in Low-Income Countries. https://blogs.imf.org/2017/06/06/protecting-education-and-health-spending-in-low-income-countries/

Leamer, E. (1983). Let's Take the Con out of Econometrics. *American Economic Review, 73,* 31–43.

Loewenson, R. (1995). Structural Adjustment and Health Policy in Africa. *International Journal of Health Services, 23,* 717–730.

Lu, C., Schneider, M. T., Gubbins, P., Leach-Kemon, K., Jamison, D., & Murray, C. J. (2010). Public Financing of Health in Developing Countries: A Cross-National Systematic Analysis. *The Lancet, 375,* 1375–1387.

Medical Express. (2009). Death Surge Linked with Mass Privatisation. https://medicalxpress.com/news/2009-01-death-surge-linked-mass-privatisation.html

Metinsoy, S. (2016, May 17). Do IMF Programmes Increase Social Spending?. https://blog.politics.ox.ac.uk/imf-programmes-increase-social-spending/

Moosa, I. A. (2012). The Failure of Financial Econometrics: "Stir-Fry" Regressions as an Illustration. *Journal of Financial Transformation, 34*, 43–50.

Moosa, I. A. (2017). *Econometrics as a Con Art: Exposing the Limitations and Abuse of Econometrics.* Cheltenham: Edward Elgar.

Nooruddin, I., & Simmons, J. W. (2006). The Politics of Hard Choices: IMF Programs and Government Spending. *International Organization, 60*, 1001–1033.

Ooms, G., & Schrecker, T. (2005). Expenditure Ceilings, Multilateral Financial Institutions, and the Health of Poor Populations. *The Lancet, 365*, 1821–1823.

Ortiz, I., Cummins, M., Capaldo, J., & Karunanethy, K. (2015). The Decade of Adjustment: A Review of Austerity Trends 2010–2020 in 187 Countries. ESS Working Papers, No. 53.

Oxfam. (1995). *The Oxfam Poverty Report.* Oxford: Oxfam.

Pitt, M. (1993). Analyzing Human Resource Effects: Health. In L. Demery, M. A. Ferroni, & C. Grootaert (Eds.), *Analyzing the Effects of Policy Reforms.* Washington, DC: World Bank.

Pollin, R., & Zhu, A. (2006). Inflation and Economic Growth: A Cross-Country Nonlinear Analysis. *Journal of Post Keynesian Economics, 28*, 593–614.

Przeworski, A., & Vreeland, J. (2000). The Effect of IMF Programs on Economic Growth. *Journal of Development Economics, 62*, 385–421.

Rowden, R. (2009a, December 11). IMF Survey: Concern over IMF Impact on Health Spending. https://www.imf.org/en/News/Articles/2015/09/28/04/53/sorea121109a

Rowden, R. (2009b). *The Deadly Ideas of Neoliberalism: How the IMF Has Undermined Public Health and the Fight against AIDS.* London: Zed Books.

Rowden, R. (2010). Doing a Decent Job? IMF Policies and Decent Work in Times of Crisis. *SOLIDAR.* http://cms.horus.be/files/99931/MediaArchive/GNreport_IMF%20and%20DW_MAIL.pdf

Sen, K., & Koivusalo, M. (1998). Health Care Reforms and Developing Countries: A Critical Overview. *International Journal of Health Planning and Management, 13*, 199–215.

Sridhar, D., & Woods, N. (2010). Are there Simple Conclusions on how to Channel Health Funding? *The Lancet, 375*, 1326–1328.

Stubbs, T., & Kentikelenis, A. (2017, February 23). How Years of IMF Prescriptions Have Hurt West African Health Systems. http://theconversation.com/how-years-of-imf-prescriptions-have-hurt-west-african-health-systems-72806

Stubbs, T., Kentikelenis, A., & King, L. (2016). Catalyzing Aid? The IMF and Donor Behavior in Aid Allocation. *World Development, 78*, 511–528.

Stubbs, T., Kentikelenis, A., Stuckler, D., McKee, M., & King, L. (2017a). The Impact of IMF Conditionality on Government Health Expenditure: A Cross-National Analysis of 16 West African Nations. *Social Science and Medicine, 174*, 220–227.

Stubbs, T., Kentikelenis, A., Stuckler, D., & McKee, M. (2017b). The IMF and Government Health Expenditure: A Response to Sanjeev Gupta. *Social Science and Medicine, 181*, 202–204.

Stuckler, D., & Basu, S. (2009). The International Monetary Fund's Effects on Global Health: Before and After the 2008 Financial Crisis. *International Journal of Health Services, 39*, 771–781.

Stuckler, D., King, L., & Basu, S. (2008). International Monetary Fund Programs and Tuberculosis Outcomes in Post-Communist Countries. *PLoS Medicine, 5*, 1079–1090.

Stuckler, D., Basu, S., & McKee, M. (2011). International Monetary Fund and Aid Displacement. *International Journal of Health Services, 41*, 67–76.

The Guardian. (2011, January 17). Poor Countries with IMF Loans Divert Aid from Public Health.

The Lancet. (2015). The International Monetary Fund and the Ebola Outbreak. *3*(2), e69–e70.

Turshen, M. (1999). *Privatizing Health Services in Africa*. New Brunswick: Rutgers University Press.

van der Hoeven, R., & Stewart, F. (1993). Social Development During Periods of Structural Adjustment in Latin America. *ILO Occasional Papers, 18*, 1–32.

Wojnilower, J. (2017). External Perspectives on the IMF and Social Protection, Background Document BD/17-01/02. International Evaluation Office.

CHAPTER 6

Keep, Reform or Abolish?

6.1 INTRODUCTION

According to Anderson (2005), the Asian financial crisis of 1997 set the stage for a debate over the role of the IMF, the organisation that promoted neoliberal policies aimed at the liberalisation of the capital account and financial markets in East Asia in the early 1990s. Those policies aggravated the situation, and as Asian countries felt the pain caused by uncontrollable capital outflows and collapsing currencies, the IMF prescribed harsh economic measures that made things worse and the pain more excruciating. A briefing paper of Oxfam (2000) suggests that "the IMF has been justifiably criticised for its response to the East Asian crisis", identifying the factors that prolonged and deepened the recession as the emphasis on demand deflation to achieve balance of payments stabilisation, the "Christmas tree" approach to loan conditions, failure to protect social sector budgets, and failure to insist on debt reduction. Likewise, Desai (2014) contends that the IMF's response to the Asian crisis of 1997 reinforced its image of being hostile to developing countries.

The IMF is looked upon differently by different people. With respect to what to do about the IMF, now that it has inflicted so much damage on developing countries, three courses of action can be distinguished. The first is that the IMF should be maintained and expanded as advocated by Eichengreen (2009) and, of course, the US Treasury as well as some observers and, naturally, the Fund itself. The second is that of restructuring and reforming the Fund, as argued by Truman (2008), the Meltzer

© The Author(s) 2019
I. A. Moosa, N. Moosa, *Eliminating the IMF*,
https://doi.org/10.1007/978-3-030-05761-9_6

Commission and others. The third course of action is to abolish the Fund as suggested, inter alia, by Bhide and Phelps (2011). Frenkel and Menkhoff (2000) contend that the IMF is "probably the most often criticized international organization" but argue that the criticism "has not harmed the IMF much but has rather demonstrated its importance in the international arena". They attribute the ineffectiveness of criticism to the fact that "demands for reform have represented opposite views and therefore also suggested changes in opposite directions". This is interpreted by the IMF and its supporters as a sign that the Fund's policy followed a middle-of-the-road path, indicating a balanced approach and characterising the Fund's critics as being "radical".

Anderson (2005) sees three alternative choices: reform, downsize or abolish, suggesting that "IMF critics loosely fall into three camps: abolitionists, progressive reformers, and the Meltzer Commission". However, she refers to critics who "fall roughly into three general categories", starting with those advocating the abolition of the IMF. These include conservatives who believe that IMF operations represent a waste of public funds, criticising IMF bailouts for eliminating the discipline of risk in private markets. It is interesting that the IMF, whose policies are based on the free-market doctrine, is criticised by free marketeers who call for its abolition.

Ironically, right-wing free marketeers are supported in their call for abolishing the IMF by people on the left who think that the abolition of the IMF would allow developing countries to pursue alternative economic policies that do not conform to the IMF's free-market prescriptions. This point has been raised by Oxfam (2000), suggesting that the stance against the IMF "unites conservative Republicans who want to rid the world of 'global government' with non-government organisations who attack the IMF for its disregard for poverty issues and transparency" and that "both regard the IMF as an abject failure". Likewise, Aiyar (1994) argues that "there has been an astonishing joining of hands by the far right, far left and deep greens, calling for the abolition of the two organisations [IMF and World Bank]". All three groups accuse the Bank and Fund of following disastrous policies that perpetuate poverty, albeit from completely different viewpoints. While right-wing observers criticise the Fund for "financing socialism in the Third World on a scale unknown in human history", those on the left claim that the Bank and Fund are "free-market maniacs".

The second camp, according to Anderson (2005), includes "labor unions, a number of environmental groups, and other progressive analysts" who want to see a curtailment of the power of the IMF to impose "draconian austerity measures", suggesting instead that the Fund should play a positive role in reducing poverty, promoting international labour and environmental standards, and placing controls on global capital flows. The third camp is represented by the recommendations of the International Financial Institutions Advisory Commission, also known as the Meltzer Commission, which was created as part of the 1998 legislation that increased the IMF's financial resources. The Commission's majority report calls for the IMF to be scaled back to serve only as a lender of last resort to solvent member governments facing liquidity crises while eliminating its power to impose conditions on developing countries in return for long-term assistance. However, it would still require that for a country to qualify for short-term assistance it must satisfy a list of rigid, free market-oriented preconditions. The US Treasury opposes the recommendations of the Meltzer Commissions in defence of the status quo.

Sometimes the debate over the IMF does not take the form of choice among keeping, reforming and abolition but rather it takes the form of raising specific questions about what should be done about the Fund. Bird (2001) summarises these issue, starting with the basic question of whether or not the world still needs the IMF. The other issues are (i) whether the IMF should be an adjustment or a lending institution; (ii) its relationship with private capital markets; (iii) whether the Fund should be a crisis averter, a crisis lender or a crisis manager; (iv) whether or not there is too much overlap with the World Bank; (v) whether or not SAPs work and the future of conditionality; (vi) transparency and governance; and (vii) how it should be financed. We will return to these points when discussing the reasons why the IMF should be abolished.

6.2   KEEPING THE IMF

Those who call for keeping the IMF, more or less as it is, argue that the status quo should be preserved because the Fund has been doing a good job. Others want to keep the Fund with minimal changes. Some even want to expand. We start with the view of the US Treasury, which supports the preservation of the status quo, a position that is motivated by the proposition that the IMF is a tool for the US Treasury to run other countries' economic affairs for the benefit of corporate USA. According to Oxfam (2000), "the proliferation of inappropriate loan conditions (i.e. opening up markets for car part manufacturers, foreign investment and foreign control of banks) reflected US Treasury demands". In fact, the requirement of capital-account liberalisation, which devastated Asian countries (and Iceland), was brought on to the Fund's agenda by two former Treasury secretaries, Robert Rubin and Larry Summers, both of whom are enthusiastic supporters of the banking industry.

Following the March 2000 release of the Meltzer Commission's report, Treasury Secretary Larry Summers denounced it, arguing that, if implemented, it would "profoundly undermine the capacity of the IMF ... and thus weaken the international financial institutions' capacity to promote central U.S. interests". In defence of the Fund, Summers claimed that without the IMF, "the [Asian] crisis would have been deeper and more protracted, with more devastating impact on the affected economies and potentially much more severe consequences for US farmers, workers, and businesses" (Oxfam 2000). This is a truly remarkable confession, which makes Summers honest in admitting that he defends the IMF because it serves US interests.

In an attempt to make it look as if the US Treasury wants to see a change in the status quo, some suggestions for "reform" were put forward, focusing on transparency and surveillance, while ignoring the problem of volatile speculative capital. According to Oxfam (2000), the Treasury Department's IMF reform plan ignores the fact that Asian countries had been following prudent economic policies prior to the crisis, and most had both low and falling inflation and budget surpluses. It was rampant speculation caused by capital-account liberalisation, and not a lack of information, that set off the Asian crisis. The Treasury's "reform plan" is silent on the need to discourage speculative capital flows. Therefore, the US Treasury effectively wants to keep things as they are for convenience.

In a debate on whether or not the IMF should be abolished, published on http://www.debate.org, most participants suggested that the IMF should be preserved. One participant suggested that the IMF should be kept because "the positive effects of this organization greatly outweigh any negative side effects". To be more specific, the IMF "serves to improve financial growth throughout the world and improve trade between countries". Another view is that "it is a greater benefit to the world to keep the Fund going" because "after World War 2, it was vital and important for the world community to make sure that countries whose economies and societies were affected by it be helped to rebuild". Yet another view is that the IMF "serves a good purpose" and "does great work around the world and helps out when there are global crises or potential global issues". Abolishing the IMF, according to this view, "would create harm". One participant in the survey believes that the IMF should be preserved because it "was founded to assist in the reconstruction of the world's international payment system after world war II", because "it provides funds (loans) on a short-term basis to all countries with payment imbalances to balance them", and because "it works to improve the economies of IMF member countries". These views are counterfactual, to say the least. The negative effects of the IMF exceed by far the positive effects, and the history of IMF operations tells us that it is not beneficial, but rather harmful, to keep the Fund going. The IMF promotes "free" trade for the benefit of the Washington preachers rather than "fair" trade for the benefit of poor countries (and no one knows what is meant by "financial growth").

Positive views of the Fund were expressed by high-profile economists and commentators in a symposium about whether or not the IMF is obsolete (International Economy 2007). In the introduction to the symposium, the following points are raised:

> Is the IMF Obsolete? Several years ago, even asking such a question would have seemed absurd. Yet today, with the narrowing of risk spreads in an era of increasingly interconnected markets and more efficient risk management, is the IMF's role still relevant? Has the rise of Asia, with its reliance on self-insurance by reserve accumulation since 1998, shown the Fund the door? The institution already once in its history, after the United States went off the gold standard, redefined its mission. Is there a need for a second round of mission redefinition? If so, what's the next mission? ... Never in the history of the world has a bureaucracy on its own shut itself down. Could this be the first time? Should it be?

Examples of the views are those of Ken Rogoff, who said that "the IMF thrives by reinventing itself", Edwin Truman who declared that "we need a leaner and meaner IMF with a different kind of staff", Alan Meltzer, who suggested that "the IMF has lost a clear sense of purpose and must reorganize", and Jeffrey Frankel who expressed the view that the IMF is needed because "success in dealing with the China currency issue requires international cooperation and multilateral surveillance". What is important is not that the IMF thrives but that the countries it is supposed to help thrive, which has not been happening. If an international body has lost a clear sense of purpose and the reason for its establishment in the first place, then the solution is not to reorganise or make it leaner but to abolish it. It is bizarre to suggest that the IMF must exist so that China can be forced not to exercise its sovereign right of adopting the exchange rate regime it deems appropriate for its economy, which is what IMF rules dictate.

Some observers believe that the IMF is still doing a good and useful job by boosting growth, dealing with financial crises, providing advice on economic and financial matters, and providing loans for countries short of liquidity. However, the facts and figures show that IMF operations are invariably detrimental to the health of the countries where it operates. The IMF's critics refer to inappropriate or dogmatic policy design (Babb and Kentikelenis 2017; Babb and Carruthers 2008; Kentikelenis et al. 2016; Stiglitz 2002), adverse effects on the economy (Dreher 2006), negative social consequences (Abouharb and Cingranelli 2007; Babb 2005; Oberdabernig 2013), and adverse effect on social spending, particularly government expenditure on health (Stubbs et al. 2017; Huber et al. 2008; Moosa 2018).

Barro (2000) holds the view that the IMF's role in the collection and distribution of data has been useful and that an advisory role might also be satisfactory. However, Barro is more in favour of abolition as he argues that this function could be performed just as well by non-governmental institutions. He also believes that the demand for the IMF's economic advice is likely to be low if it is no longer tied to its loans. Recent history, however, tells us that the IMF's advice brought havoc on the countries going by the advice as a condition for getting loans. Who wants this kind of advice when even the countries that had to follow the advice found it tantalising to get out of it?

Some economists even call for expansion in the role played by the IMF. Eichengreen (2009) suggests what he calls a "more ambitious reforms of the international financial architecture", including expansion of IMF quotas and the conduct of exchange rate surveillance, as well as an expanded role for the SDR in international transactions, which would require the IMF to act as market maker. Exchange rate surveillance should be unnecessary, given that the Jamaica Accord allows any country to adopt any exchange rate arrangement it deems appropriate for its economy. It seems, however, that a measure like this is intended against China, which has been accused of manipulating its currency (Moosa 2012). While Eichengreen makes the good proposal of re-imposing "Glass-Steagall-like restrictions on commercial and investment banking", such that the IMF acts as an international co-ordinator in this respect, this role is unlikely to be allowed by bankers who always win. He also suggests that banks should be required to purchase capital insurance, with the IMF acting on the other side of the market.

More tasks are proposed for the IMF, including cross-border bank insolvencies and the power to sanction members whose national regulatory policies are not up to "international standards". This sounds much like what the Basel Committee on Banking Supervision (BCBS) is supposed to do, but the BCBS does not have the power to impose anything on any member country. It sounds ludicrous to suggest that an organisation that has failed miserably in fulfilling its declared objectives should be given more powers. But then perhaps the IMF work has not been a failure but rather a spectacular success when it comes to doing things for the benefit of the beneficiaries.

6.3   Reforming the IMF

In contrast to those who think that that the IMF should be preserved, as it is or with some cosmetic changes, some observers believe that the IMF can only be kept with a significant reform. For example, Akyüz (2005) suggests that the Fund needs reforming in order to retain, or rather restore, its relevance and credibility and that the Fund needs to reinvent itself. For example, he argues that "there is no sound rationale for it to be involved in development matters, including long-term lending" and that "the Fund should pay much greater attention to two areas in which its existence carries a stronger rationale; namely, short-term counter-cyclical current account financing, and effective surveillance over national macroeconomic and financial policies, particularly of countries which have a disproportionately large impact on international monetary and financial stability". In other words, he argues, a genuine reform of the Fund would require as much a redirection of its activities as improvements in its policies and operational modalities. Addressing these issues would not be possible without dealing with shortcomings in its governance structure.

The majority report of the Meltzer Commission (signed by 8 of 11 members) recommends the termination of long-term IMF assistance tied to conditions on the grounds that conditionality and SAPs have caused suffering for millions of people around the world. The conditionality associated with long-term assistance is to be replaced with conditionality associated with short-term (120 days maximum) crisis assistance. For a country to become eligible for short-term assistance, it must satisfy the following preconditions: (i) freedom of entry and operation for foreign financial institutions; (ii) adequately capitalised commercial banks as recommended by the BCBS; and (iii) a proper fiscal requirement to make sure that IMF resources would not be used to sustain "irresponsible budget policies".

The first precondition is very much in the spirit of the Washington Consensus, allowing predatory foreign financial institutions to run their Ponzi schemes without being subject to any kind of regulation. The second requirement of following the guidelines set by the BCBS does not serve any purpose and can be harmful for at least two reasons: (i) the Basel rules are problematic, they make the banking industry even more procyclical than otherwise, and they deprive small and medium enterprises of credit; and (ii) applying the same rules to banking in developed and developing countries, in the spirit of unification of banking rules, is not such a good idea. The problem with the third condition is that it gives the IMF the power to define "irresponsible" while keeping up the tradition of forcing governments to slash spending on social programmes. At one time, the IMF was critical of Sweden (a country with low inflation, remarkable productivity growth and falling unemployment) for providing generous unemployment insurance. This is conditionality all over again applied to short-term lending—no conditionality is applied to long-term lending because long-term lending is to be abolished. If a country is announced as being "irresponsible", if it fails to meet the Basel rules, or if it does something that makes it inconvenient for foreign financial institutions to run their Ponzi schemes, the country will be excluded from the privilege of obtaining financial assistance from the Fund. That will also affect its credit rating and make it difficult for that country to tap international financial markets.

Anderson (2005) acknowledges "the most positive contribution of the Meltzer Report", which is a recommendation for the cancellation of all debts to the heavily indebted poorest countries. However, the cancellation is subject to the condition that the underlying country has an approved "economic development strategy", invariably based on the ten commandments of the Washington Consensus. What is the point of placing conditions on debts that, according to the Commission, cannot be repaid anyway? A more logical course of action is unconditional cancellation.

Oxfam (2000) is rather critical of the Meltzer report because it calls for the Fund to depart low-income countries and focus on crisis prevention in financial markets, expressing concern for the following reasons: (i) it reflects a growing disenchantment with multilateralism; (ii) it threatens to replace inappropriate IMF conditions with inappropriate conditions dictated by the

G7 countries; (iii) it fails to address the real policy issues at the heart of the IMF's failure as a poverty reduction agency; (iv) it does not address the politicisation of IMF loans, particularly with respect to the influence of the US Treasury; and (v) it does not consider adequately the "democratic deficit" that prevents poor countries from having an effective voice in the IMF. Oxfam (2000) believes that the IMF has failed to address the challenge of developing a poverty-focused approach to macroeconomic stabilisation, that it is remote, unaccountable and undemocratic, and that it suffers from "mission creep on a grand scale". The Oxfam report is blunt, referring to "inappropriate policy conditions being applied in areas where Fund staff are ill-qualified" and suggesting that "the US and the G7 have got the IMF they want" because they control 57% of the vote. Thus, the IMF is described as a "financial institution comprising structural creditors, who dictate loan conditions, and structural debtors, who accept the said conditions".

Oxfam (2000) makes the following recommendations for IMF reform: (i) abandoning the current stabilisation model, in favour of a more expansionary fiscal framework; (ii) ensuring that budget provisions are consistent with poverty reduction strategies; (iii) paying more attention to the sequencing of reforms, which is the same point raised by Stiglitz (2002); and (iv) abandoning conditions in areas such as privatisation and trade liberalisation. For the IMF itself, however, all is fine and the reform has already been implemented. In a report written by own staff, the IMF (2000) spells how it has been engaged in a process of reform "over the past several years"—the motivation being "the need to adapt to the challenges of the global economy". Those claims were basically made by Managing Director Horst Köhler to the IMF Board of Governors at the IMF-World Bank Annual Meetings held in Prague in September 2000. In his speech, Köhler specified what had been done thus far and outlined six areas where further change was needed: (i) strengthening surveillance and crisis prevention, (ii) helping member countries strengthen their institutional capacity, (iii) improving IMF lending by streamlining conditionality, (iv) enhancing the framework for crisis resolution, (v) strengthening support for low-income countries and (vi) increasing transparency and accountability.

Another set of proposed reforms have been put forward by Truman (2008) as follows: (i) substantial progress on IMF governance, (ii) greater attention to the policies of a broader group of systematically important countries, (iii) re-establishing the central role of the Fund in external financial crises, (iv) refocused engagement with low-income members,

(v) attention to the capital account and financial sector, and (vi) the need for additional financial resources. A thorough reading of these proposals reveals that they are intended to give the IMF renewed legitimacy without changing the status quo in a substantial manner. For example, Truman suggests that countries other than the G7 should have a bigger say in IMF affairs, effectively the replacement of 7 tyrants with 15 tyrants. It remains to say that Edwin Truman was Assistant Secretary of the Treasury for International Affairs during the period 1998–2000.

The IMF, it is claimed, strives to improve governance in all member countries, in which case "the IMF should expand its dialogue with the public and reach out, not least to civil society". To accomplish this objective, the IMF staff are instructed to meet with civil society organisations, including non-governmental organisations, and labour and religious groups. These meetings often take the form of seminars and briefings organised by the IMF on topics that are of particular interest to the civil society. So, it is all about the IMF telling those groups what the IMF is going to do, in an exercise of self-glorification. Participants in the seminars are expected to listen and nod in agreement. And then if the IMF is concerned about governance, it should start with its own governance. The IMF, it is claimed, "should take into account the difficulties emerging market and developing countries may encounter when implementing internationally recognized standards and codes". For this purpose, the IMF started to provide benchmarks of "good practice" to improve "the quality of policy making and investment decisions". The problem is that the IMF determines what falls under "good practice", which would invariably include the holy trinity of privatisation, liberalisation and deregulation. This is why in the same document emphasis is placed on "market-oriented solutions". This is not reform—it is business as usual.

6.4   Abolishing the IMF: Take One

Those calling for abolishing the IMF argue on two grounds. The first is that the IMF should be abolished because the purpose for which it was created no longer exists. The second is that it should be abolished because it has done a lot of damage and inflicted misery on the people of the countries unfortunate enough to receive aid and get exposed to the tyranny of conditionality and SAPs. For example, Akyüz (2005) suggests that several observers (including former Treasury Secretaries of the United States, a Nobel Prize economist and many NGOs) have called for its abolition on the grounds that it is no longer needed, or that its interventions in emerging market crises are not only wasteful but also harmful for international economic stability, or that its adjustment programmes in poor countries aggravate rather than alleviate poverty. In this section we discuss the proposition that the IMF should be abolished because it is no longer needed for the purpose it was established for.

The IMF was established in 1944 to supervise the Bretton Woods system of fixed but adjustable exchange rates. The system collapsed in 1971 when the convertibility of the dollar into gold, a pillar of the Bretton Woods System, was abolished. With the collapse of the system, the very reason for the existence of the IMF was no longer there, which makes it plausible to suggest that the Fund should have been abolished then. However, the IMF has reinvented itself as a development agency, assuming functions that were originally assigned to the World Bank. Since then it has been in business as usual—actually, business as more than usual as the organisation has become bigger and richer. This is how Kain (2011) describes the situation:

> Undeterred by the total disappearance of its purpose, the IMF—flush with continuing streams of subsidies, especially from American taxpayers—morphed into a "development" agency. The quotation marks around "development" are no mistake. There's no evidence that the IMF's efforts as a development agency have had any positive effects, unless by "positive effects" you include creating among many poor countries a culture of dependency upon foreign "aid", along with propping up authoritarian regimes.

Likewise, Friedman (1998) argued that "the IMF lost its only function and should have closed shop". Kain (2011) cites Leland Yeager as saying that "self-important international bureaucracies have institutional incentives to invent new functions for themselves, to expand, and to keep client countries dependent on their aid" (Yeager 1998). Kain goes on to say that "the IMF skilfully used a series of global economic crises to increase its capital base and financing activities"—these crises include the oil crisis of the 1970s, the debt crisis of the 1980s, transformation of the former communist countries in the early 1990s, and the Mexican, East Asian and Russian financial crises in the mid- to late 1990s. Bird (2003) suggests that "with flexible exchange rates and mobile international capital it is no longer needed". Bird (2001) elaborates on this issue as follows:

During the 1970s the IMF became marginalized as an institution. Its adjustment role was reduced by the introduction of exchange rate flexibility. Its lending role was overshadowed by international financial intermediation by the private banks. Its macroeconomic co-ordination role seemed less relevant where it was believed that flexible exchange rates would insulate countries from external shocks. Even its role as a forum for international monetary reform was reduced by the trend towards regionalization in Europe and the existence of other fora with overlapping spheres of responsibility.

Akyüz (2005) expresses a similar view by saying:

The Fund is no longer performing the tasks it was originally created for. It started out as an institution to promote global stability through multilateral discipline over exchange rate policies, control over capital flows and provision of short-term liquidity for trade financing. It has ended up focussing, on the one hand, on development issues, providing long-term financing on concessional terms and, on the other hand, on the management of capital-account crises associated with instability of capital flows, allocating a large proportion of its resources for financing capital outflows.

Oxfam (2000) puts forward the following argument:

The IMF has lacked a proper role since 1971, when the exchange rate system it was created to oversee collapsed (that is, the Bretton Woods system). For the past three decades it has been an institution in search of a role. It has mishandled virtually every crisis since acting as a debt collection agency for commercial banks in the 1980s—and it has singularly failed to advance the cause of poverty reduction and equity.

Desai (2014) agrees by saying the following:

The IMF had taken upon itself to monitor financial stability as a new task in the first decade of the 21st century. One can only say that it failed miserably in either forewarning or preventing the financial crisis when it came. The IMF has also taken on the task of being a macroeconomic forecaster for its members. Here again, the performance is not great as was shown by the debacle concerning the UK's austerity policies, something which the IMF misread completely.

Reinhart and Trebesch (2016) consider how the IMF has reinvented itself, suggesting that

A sketch of the International Monetary Fund's 70-year history reveals an institution that has reinvented itself over time along multiple dimensions. ... Some deceptively "new" IMF activities are not entirely new. ... While currency problems were the dominant trigger of IMF involvement in the earlier decades, banking crises and sovereign defaults became the key focus since the 1980s. Around this time, the IMF shifted from providing relatively brief (and comparatively modest) balance-of-payments support in the era of fixed exchange rates to coping with more chronic debt sustainability problems that emerged with force in the developing nations and now migrated to advanced ones. ... We conclude that these practices impair the IMF's role as an international lender of last resort.

Bhide and Phelps (2011) suggest that bold reforms transformed emerging economies, such as BRICS (Brazil, Russia, India, China and South Africa), nearly put the IMF out of business, which by 2008 was struggling with its own budget deficit of $400 million. Truman shares the sentiment by suggesting that "in the first decade of the 21st century the IMF faced crises of legitimacy, relevance and budgetary finance". What saved the IMF then, according to them, was PIGS (Portugal, Ireland, Greece and Spain), the countries that put themselves in trouble by following the ten commandments of the Washington Consensus and financialising their economies to the extreme.

It may be argued that the alternative to abolishing the IMF for this reason is to merge it with the World Bank because they are doing pretty much the same thing with the same "customers". The problem is that nothing will change as they are equally brutal in terms of conditionality and SAPs. Whatever is said about the IMF is equally applicable to the World Bank. However, if the combined institution becomes a genuine development agency, that will be an option, but this is unwarranted optimism. Oxfam (2000) believes that simply abolishing the Fund would not necessarily change the policy environment. At best, Oxfam says, it would lead to major donors finding new mechanisms for imposing the same conditions that they currently insist on through the Fund.

6.5   ABOLISHING THE FUND: TAKE TWO

Calls for abolishing the Fund may be based on an evaluation in terms of costs and benefits. For those wanting to see it vanish, the Fund has caused extensive damage and very little benefit for the wider community. In this section we consider the adverse consequences of IMF operations that have become quite conspicuous. They are not listed in any particular order, and overlapping is inevitable.

A Force for Good?

Hanke (2000) argues that "the IMF's policies don't generate prosperity or alleviate poverty". Gauding (2011) suggests that the general public holds the vague idea that the IMF is a force for good, helping developing countries with loans and other assistance to improve their economies. In reality, he argues, the IMF is the "prime cause of increased poverty and suffering around the globe".

The IMF is seen as being out there to benefit bankers and multinationals by giving them access to markets and would-be-privatised public assets in the countries that are unlucky enough to get "help" from the Fund. Krishnan (2016) suggests that while the IMF claims to do good by making stringent policies and offering stability, it has through the years "systematically crippled world economies in favour of large multinational corporations and wealthy private investors". To increase exports, countries are encouraged (by the IMF) to give tax breaks and subsidies to export industries. Public assets such as forest-land and government utilities (telephone, water and electricity companies) are sold off to foreign investors at rock bottom prices. In Guyana, a foreign timber company called Barama received an extensive logging concession as well as a five-year tax holiday (so much for the objective of boosting tax revenue that the IMF advocates). The IMF forced Haiti to open its market to imported, highly subsidised US rice while prohibiting subsidies to farmers. A US corporation called Early Rice now sells nearly 50% of the rice consumed in Haiti.

It is also believed that IMF operations have a negative impact on access to food and the environment. According to Oxfam (2002), "a number of civil society organisations have criticised the IMF's policies for their impact on access to food, particularly in developing countries". More specifically, Oxfam points out that 13 million people face severe food shortages and famine in southern Africa, attributing the situation in part to "the failure of 15 years of agricultural growth and food security".

The IMF makes it difficult for indebted countries to reject environmentally harmful projects that nevertheless generate revenues such as oil, coal and forest-destroying lumber and agriculture projects. IMF operations invariably lead to the exploitation of natural resources on a massive scale, without any consideration of the environmental ramifications as the main objective is boosting exports to earn hard currency that is used to pay back loans. For example, Côte d'Ivoire's increased reliance on cocoa exports has led to a loss of two-thirds of the country's forests. We have also seen that the IMF has a depressing effect on social expenditure.

The Macroeconomic and Welfare Effects of IMF Operations

The empirical evidence on the macroeconomic and welfare effects of IMF operations is not that sanguine from the IMF's perspective. Khan (1990), who was for a long time a senior member of the Fund's staff, conducts a comprehensive assessment of the impact of IMF policies on macroeconomic variables such as the current account, inflation and growth. After reviewing 13 studies covering the Fund's activities from 1963 to 1982, he concludes that (i) there is frequently an improvement in the balance of payments, although a number of studies show no effects; (ii) inflation is generally not affected by IMF programmes; and (iii) the effects on the growth rate are uncertain.

Likewise, Johnson and Schaefer (1997) examine the relation between IMF loans and economic growth in less-developed countries from 1965 through 1995 and find that 48 of the 89 loan recipients were not better off in 1995 (as measured by real per capita wealth) than before they accepted their first loan, that 32 of those 48 countries were poorer, and that 14 of the 32 countries had economies that were at least 15% smaller than what they were before their first loan. For example, Nicaragua received $185 million from the IMF between 1968 and 1995, yet its economy contracted 55%. Zaire received $1.8 billion between 1972 and 1995, and its economy contracted 54%.

Long-Term IMF Dependence

Bandow (1994) examined the Fund's financing activities from 1947 through 1989 and found that six countries relied on IMF assistance for more than 30 years, 24 countries for 20–29 years, and 47 countries for 10–19 years. Of the 83 developing countries that used IMF resources for at least 60% of the years since they started borrowing, more than half have relied on the IMF every year. Bird (1995) concludes that "the image of the Fund coming into a country, offering swift financial support, helping to turn the balance of payments around, and then getting out, is purely and simply wrong". In effect the Fund becomes something like a colonial force.

Ben-Ami (2011) argues that the IMF helps absolve politicians of their responsibility. One reason why politicians often opt for IMF bailouts in times of trouble is that it provides them with a way of evading responsibility for their actions. They can claim that austerity is imposed by an external institution, which they accept reluctantly for fear of losing access to the Fund's resources. Furthermore, corrupt politicians typically benefit from the work of the IMF at the expense of a starving population. The abolition of the IMF would make the culpability of corrupt politicians more transparent.

Support of Dictatorships

The IMF is generally apathetic or hostile to human rights, providing support for military dictatorships if they are friendly to "western" corporations. The Fund supported Mobutu's rule in Zaire, although its own envoy, Erwin Blumenthal, provided a sobering report about the entrenched corruption and embezzlement and the inability of the country to pay back its debt (van Reybrouck 2012). Blumenthal resigned from his position at Zaire's central bank in 1980, complaining about "sordid and pernicious corruption". The corruption was so serious that Blumenthal declared: "there is no chance, I repeat no chance, that Zaire's numerous creditors will ever recover their loans". As Mobutu became one of the world's richest people, the "west" and the IMF saw him as a loyal ally in the Cold War as he supported the US in its backing for the National Union for the Total Independence of Angola (UNITA).

Adusei (2009) refers to the "poor people of Indonesia" who are still paying for the billions of dollars wasted before the eyes of the IMF. Indonesia received a total of $30 billion in loans during General Suharto's three decades of rule. In 1998, World Bank resident staff in Indonesia estimated that at least 20% (perhaps as high as 30%) of Indonesia's development budget funds were diverted to private accounts. Absolutely nothing was done to put an end to corruption. During the regime of the dictator Ferdinand Marcos in the Philippines, the IMF knew that most loans were transferred into the bank accounts of Marcos and his generals, but that was seen as a "necessary bribe" to ensure the acceleration of "reform", the privatisation, liberalisation and deregulation kind of reform. Marcos also received $80 million in kickbacks from Westinghouse in return for winning a $2.3 billion contract to build the Bataan nuclear plant.

Supporting dictatorships has always been a game played by imperialist forces for the benefit of big companies that get lucrative projects. Offering bribes and kickbacks to corrupt officials in developing countries is a common practice, which is even justified in the name of efficiency and cutting red-tape. As a tool of the governments of the "west", the US in particular, the IMF is known to have participated in this game.

Moral Hazard

The IMF's implicit guarantee of subsidised bailouts reduces the cost of fiscally irresponsible yet rewarding policies that encourage even greater recklessness. This constitutes moral hazard, which was evident in July 1998 when Russia promised to implement key economic policies in exchange for an $11.2 billion IMF loan commitment. The Yeltsin government abandoned its commitments, devalued the ruble, defaulted on its debt, began printing money excessively, fired almost every reformer in the government and failed to enact many of the promised reforms. But Yeltsin was the darling of the "west", which is why IMF loans to Russia were pushed by the Clinton State Department. The same story goes for the 1995 IMF bailout of investors in Mexico.

Inappropriate Loan Conditions

IMF policy prescriptions are usually "off-the-shelf" remedies that are not adequately tailored to each country's unique circumstances—these conditions typically prolong and deepen financial crises. For example, the IMF failed to recognise that the East Asian crisis was a banking crisis, not a fiscal crisis, which made its traditional prescriptions inappropriate and exacerbated the problem. Hanke (1998) summarises the debacle as follows:

> The International Monetary Fund failed to anticipate Asia's financial crisis. Then, to add insult to injury, the IMF misdiagnosed the patient's malady and prescribed the wrong medicine. Not surprisingly, the patient's condition has gone from bad to worse. Perhaps it is best, therefore, that governments seldom honor the terms of their loan agreements.

Gauding (2011) tells a story of how the IMF caused starvation in Malawi as presented by Johann Hari. During the 1990s, Malawi was facing severe economic problems due to a terrible HIV/AIDS epidemic and a horrific dictatorship. When the Malawi government requested help, the IMF demanded the imposition of a structural adjustment programme. As a result, the government was told to sell off public assets to private companies and speculators and to put an end to subsidies. Particularly devastating was the abolition of fertiliser subsidies, even though those subsidies made it possible for farmers to grow food in the country's depleted soil. Furthermore, the IMF wanted available funds to be used to repay international bankers rather than help the Malawian people. In 2001, when the IMF found out that the Malawian government had built up large stockpiles of grain in case of a crop failure, the government was ordered to sell off those stockpiles to private companies so that the proceeds could be used to pay off an IMF-recommended loan from a large bank, a loan that carried a 56% annual interest. In the following year the crops failed, causing starvation—yet the IMF suspended $47 million in aid because the government was not enacting the free-market adjustments fast enough.

In 2005, at the height of the starvation and economic wreckage caused by the IMF, Malawi ignored the Fund's instructions and re-introduced fertiliser subsidies, along with a range of other services to ordinary people. Subsequently, Malawi was not only able to feed its population, but it also began to provide food aid to Uganda and Zimbabwe. In her article "Ending famine simply by ignoring the Experts", Dugger (2007) wrote the following:

> This year, a nation that has perennially extended a begging bowl to the world is instead feeding its hungry neighbors. It is selling more corn to the World Food Program of the United Nations than any other country in southern Africa and is exporting hundreds of thousands of tons of corn to Zimbabwe.

There is more where this came from. In Kenya, one of the worst-affected countries by AIDS, the IMF insisted on the introduction of fees to see doctors, thus exacerbating the epidemic. In Ghana, the IMF insisted on the introduction of school fees, exacerbating illiteracy. In Zambia, the IMF insisted on slashing health spending, and hence the number of babies who died prematurely doubled. All of this happened while those countries were required to keep foreign bankers and multinationals happy.

Conditionality Compliance and Enforcement

It is impossible for outsiders to monitor conditionality compliance routinely since loan terms and data are confidential and released only voluntarily. Edwards (1989) examined the degree of compliance by using the Fund's own data, looking at the compliance rate for 34 programmes that were approved in 1983 in response to the international debt crisis. He found the median compliance rate with IMF loan conditions between 1983 and 1985 to be only 46%. The compliance rate for government deficit never reached this level once and was 19% in 1984. Meanwhile, the median compliance rate for targets pertaining to the current account, inflation and economic growth was only 41%. Sachs (1989) concludes that "the evidence presented in the IMF's 1988 review of conditionality … suggests that, since 1983, the rate of compliance has been decreasing sharply, down to less than one-third compliance with program performance criteria in the most recent years".

Discrimination and Opacity

Ben-Ami (2011) argues that "the IMF has functioned more like a medieval court than a modern organisation". Owing to a long-standing agreement among "western" countries, the IMF is typically headed by a European, while the World Bank is headed by an American. The appointees, according to Ben-Ami (2011), "have never been chosen by merit" and "will be chosen in a backroom deal between a few top politicians rather than going through a transparent or democratic process". Barro (2000) describes the appointment of the IMF's managing director as a "circus-like process". This is what he says in this respect:

> After a lengthy public debate, the leading countries settled on another German, Horst Köhler, to replace Michel Camdessus as the IMF's managing director. Unfortunately, the circus-like process began to resemble an affirmative-action procedure when it became clear that a particular nationality-German-was a prerequisite for the job.

Unfortunately, Barro's alternative to the "circus-like process" and "affirmative-action procedure" would have been to appoint Stanley Fischer, who was deputy managing director at the time. Three years later, it was Stanley Fischer who insisted on privatisation and the removal of subsidies in occupied Iraq. However, one has to be fair and acknowledge the fact that Barro is in favour of abolishing the Fund as he expressed his unfavourable opinion of the IMF's social value and his surprise that the Meltzer Commission did not advocate the abolition of the IMF.

The IMF operates as a secretive organisation without accountability, and even though it is funded with taxpayer money, it operates behind a veil of secrecy. Members of affected communities do not participate in designing loan packages. The IMF works with a select group of central bankers and finance ministers to make policies without input from other government agencies such as health, education and environment departments. As mentioned previously, the IMF claims that it is now meeting with various sectors of the civil society, but only to tell them that "this is what we are going to do and this is how we are going to do it".

Furthermore, the prescribed policies are often discriminatory against developing countries—for example, the IMF gave rich countries considerable leeway to pursue fiscal stimulus in the aftermath of the global financial crisis, but immediate austerity was prescribed as a solution to the Asian financial crisis. Gauding (2011) argues that the IMF is "inconsistent", because it supports huge state-funded bank bailouts in the rich world, while demanding an end to almost all state funding in the poor world.

Governance Issues

The IMF's membership is divided along income lines: certain countries provide the financial resources (developed countries) while others use these resources (developing countries). Tension is created around governance issues because these two groups, creditors and borrowers, have fundamentally different interests. The system of voting power distribution through a quota system institutionalises borrower subordination and creditor dominance.

Unlike a democratic system in which each member country would have an equal vote, rich countries dominate decision-making in the IMF because voting power is determined by the amount of money that each country pays into the quota system. Torres (2007), who wonders if votes for money is a good idea, suggests that the governance structure of the IMF is "inconsistent with its multilateral nature and is dysfunctional to its purpose". The US is the largest shareholder with a quota of 18%. Germany, Japan, France, the UK and the US combined control about 38%. The disproportionate amount of power held by rich countries means that the interests of bankers, investors and corporations from these countries are put above the needs of the world's poor majority. As Torres (2007) puts it, "fat cats come first". Bird (2001) discusses the view that the Fund has become overly political, in the sense that lending decisions are forced through by creditor countries with the objective of preventing specific debtor countries from defaulting and thereby damaging the interests of large commercial banks.

Excessive US Influence

The way the IMF is set up gives the US a veto on any action that it disapproves because it holds a big voting power. The influence of the US even reaches into decision-making concerning individual loan agreements (Oatley and Yackee 2004). The US has historically been openly opposed to losing what Treasury Secretary Jacob Lew described in 2015 as its "leadership role" at the IMF and its "ability to shape international norms and practices" (Donnan and Dyer 2015).

In July 2018, the news came that the government of Ecuador was considering the eviction of Julian Assange from the Ecuadorian embassy in London, with the intention of turning him over to the British authorities and perhaps eventually to the US authorities. On 24 July, Lenin Moreno, the newly elected President of Ecuador, arrived in London to give a speech at the Global Disability Summit 2018, but media reports suggested that the actual purpose of his visit was to finalise a deal with the British government to withdraw its asylum protection of Assange. Kumar (2018) quotes "sources close to Assange" as saying that Assange was not aware of the talks but believed that the US was putting "significant pressure" on Ecuador, including threatening to block a loan from the IMF, if Assange continues to stay at the embassy.

Short-Termism

The IMF policies are characterised by short-termism, preferring short-term financial stability over long-term growth. This is one reason why the post-crisis world economy has been characterised by weak growth, with little attempt to address the problem. Ben-Ami (2011) argues that IMF bailout programmes are aimed at rescuing troubled financial institutions, under the notorious pretext of too big to fail, rather than helping national economies return to growth. In a sense, the IMF programmes resemble what Ben-Ami (2011) describes as a "kind of institutional welfare programme".

Interference in Domestic Politics

Hanke (2000) suggests that "the International Monetary Fund interferes too much in the domestic politics of the countries it seeks to assist". As an example he tells the story of President Suharto, who was not a popular man with the IMF or the Clinton Administration. When he wanted to stabilise the rupiah by establishing a currency board (on advice from Hanke), the IMF and the Administration mounted a massive counterattack, pressuring the Indonesian government to back off the board idea. On his retirement, a former IMF managing director, Michel Camdessus, boasted that "we created the conditions that obliged President Suharto to leave his job". In other words, Hanke argues, "they caused considerable human suffering in the course of trying to accomplish a political goal". Former Tanzanian President Julius Nyerere, who thought that debt-ridden African states were ceding sovereignty to the IMF and the World Bank, wondered "who elected the IMF to be the ministry of finance for every country in the world?" (Mwakikagile 2006).

The IMF has consistently undermined the ability of democratic governments to set their own priorities and policy objectives by forcing them to go through "shock therapy" without adequate legislative or democratic processes. Nelson and Wallace (2017) outline several pathways through which IMF programme participation might affect the levels of democracy in borrowing countries and suggest the possibility of a positive association between lending programme participation and democracy scores. When democracy is undermined and governments are unable to act in the interest of their electorate, one of the only channels left is for citizens to demonstrate. Civil unrest, demonstrations and strikes should indicate to governments, law-makers and the international community that policies are not working. Metinsoy and Angin (2017) argue that when the power of the borrowing government vis-à-vis the IMF declines, the likelihood of an adverse impact on the representative institutions and the probability that they will be bypassed increases. They demonstrate this proposition with reference to Greece over the period between 2010 and 2015, showing that whenever the borrowing government is weak vis-à-vis the IMF and there is a disagreement between the governing party and the Fund, IMF programmes curtail the representative function of democratic institutions.

The Burden of Debt

Adusei (2009) points out that developing countries have incurred trillions of dollars in debt through loans contracted from the Bank, IMF and "western" governments from which the people who now wallow in utter poverty never benefited. Most of the conditional loans were either stolen or used to service existing debt. Part of the loans was also used to pay foreign expatriates supplied to the poor countries by the IMF and World Bank as "technical experts".

The servicing of massive debt has brought untold and worsening economic hardship to the poor in recipient countries as governments are forced to freeze investment in education, health, transport, agriculture, housing, sanitation and infrastructure. Indicative of hardship are chronic poverty, malnutrition, diseases, starvation, hunger, decaying and inadequate infrastructure, and economic failure, which are symptomatic of developing world countries. What is more tragic is that the current generation bears the burden of paying back loans that they never requested or benefited from. On the situation in Africa, Adusei (2009) suggests the following:

> The albatross of illegitimate debt diverts money directly from spending on health care, education and other important needs. While most people in Africa live on less than $2 per day, African countries are forced to spend almost $14 billion each year servicing old, illegitimate debts to rich country governments and their institutions, the World Bank and the International Monetary Fund (IMF). Over the past two decades, African countries have paid out more in debt service to foreign creditors than they have received in development assistance or in new loans. Much of Africa's foreign debt is illegitimate in nature, having been incurred by unrepresentative and despotic regimes, mainly during the era of Cold War patronage. Loans were made to corrupt leaders who used the money for their own personal gain, often with the full knowledge and support of lenders. These loans did not benefit Africa's people.

Adusei (2009) suggests that "instead of being agents of growth, development and helping to fight poverty, what the two institutions [IMF and World Bank] and their western political masters have done so far is to entrench poverty, diseases, hunger, starvation and malnutrition in these poor voiceless countries". He also argues that poor countries are put under pressure to use scarce resources to service debt to the detriment of their economies and their peoples.

The Effect on Workers and Women

The IMF frequently advises countries to attract foreign investors by weakening their labour laws, such as those governing collective bargaining, and making labour markets more flexible by allowing foreign companies to fire workers at will and pay minimal wages. For example, the government of Haiti was urged to change the labour code that required increasing the minimum wage when inflation exceeded 10%. By the end of 1997, Haiti's minimum wage was only $2.40 a day, making it a source of cheap labour. This affected not only workers in Haiti but also workers in the US who had to compete with cheap, exploited labour. The IMF's handling of the Asian financial crisis led to deep depression in the affected countries, creating millions of "newly poor". Sweatshop workers in the free trade zones set up by the IMF earn starvation wages and live in deplorable conditions.

IMF policies make it difficult for women to meet their families' basic needs. The IMF typically recommends the imposition of fees for the use of public services such as health and education. As a result, girls are the first to be withdrawn from school to save the cost of education. The same policy makes healthcare unaffordable to those who need it most. The shift of emphasis to exports makes agricultural products more expensive and therefore it becomes more difficult for women to feed their families. Weak labour laws affect women who are exploited and abused in sweatshops.

Financial Crises

One of the major causes of the global financial crisis was financial deregulation, which is a typical recommendation of the IMF. Financial deregulation leads to rampant speculation in the financial markets of developing countries, attracting short-term capital. It is believed that the Mexican 1995 peso crisis was partly a result of IMF-prescribed policies. During the bailout of Asian countries, the IMF required governments to assume the bad debts of private banks, thus making the public pay the costs and draining yet more resources away from social programmes. Still, IMF intervention does not put an end to financial panic, causing financial contagion as a crisis spreads to more countries. Following the implementation of IMF-prescribed policies in response to the Mexican crisis of 1995, the number of Mexicans living in extreme poverty went up while the national average minimum wage fell significantly.

The Imposition of a Fundamentally Flawed Development Model

Unlike the path historically followed by industrialised countries, the IMF forces developing countries in need of financial assistance to prioritise export production over the development of diversified domestic economies. Forcing farmers to shift from the production of food for local consumption to the production of export crops destined for "western" countries is the major cause of malnourishment that affects children in particular. The IMF also requires countries to eliminate subsidies to domestic industry while providing benefits for and granting concessions to multinational corporations. As a result, small businesses and farmers cannot compete and go out of business. The cycle of poverty is perpetuated, not eliminated, as governments' debt to the IMF grows.

Bhide and Phelps (2011) refer to what they call the IMF's business model that sabotaged "properly functioning capitalism", victimising ordinary people while benefiting the elite. A properly functioning capitalism requires regulation and government intervention unlike laissez-faire. Stiglitz (2002) argues that the IMF ignores the implications of incomplete information, inadequate markets and unworkable institutions, all of which are characteristics of developing countries. Under these conditions the invisible hand does not work and outcomes can be improved by "well-chosen interventions".

6.6   Concluding Remarks

So, what should be done about the IMF: keep as is, reform or abolish? Given the damage that has been inflicted on developing countries by following IMF-prescribed policies over many years, the option of maintaining the status quo is a non-starter. Reform has been suggested in various shapes and forms; some are cosmetic while others are more fundamental yet inadequate for changing the status quo. Those who want to maintain the status quo or implement cosmetic changes are the IMF staff and the beneficiary of IMF operations. According to Krishnan (2016), "the deal makers and high ranking members of the IMF and World Bank get considerably well paid when acting in favour of these multinational entities". Even right-wing free marketeers want to see the IMF abolished, albeit for the wrong reason. Two fundamental reasons can be presented for the desire to abolish the IMF. The first is that the Fund is no longer serving any meaningful purpose, now that the purpose for which it was established in the first place no longer exists. The second is that it is not viable in terms of costs and benefits.

Krishnan (2016) believes that the IMF is a tool for wealthy investors and multinational corporations to execute their corporate agendas, in the process perpetuating worldwide poverty, income inequality and the exploitation of developing countries. He also believes that "it is foolish to concentrate so much power in the hands of a handful of like-minded neoliberalist people who are ruthless and blinded by their thoughtless pursuit of power and dollar signs at the expense of the rest of the world". With the IMF, countries cannot get rid of debt, and income inequality will remain the rule rather than the exception. According to Krishnan (2016), the facade of the IMF and World Bank as neutral entities is "flawed in every way especially when they have only the interests of the trans-national organizations and themselves in mind".

What is the alternative to the IMF, one may ask? Well, any alternative is better than the tyranny of IMF-prescribed plans. This is why Bhide and Phelps (2011) wonder if we need international agencies to enable "irresponsible, verging on immoral, lending and borrowing". However, alternative organisations have already been proposed. In March 2011 the ministers of economy and finance of the African Union proposed the establishment of an African Monetary Fund. At the 6th BRICS summit in July 2014, the BRICS nations (Brazil, Russia, India, China and South Africa) announced the BRICS Contingent Reserve Arrangement (CRA) with an initial size of $100 billion, a framework to provide liquidity through currency swaps in response to actual or potential short-term balance-of-payments pressures. And in 2014, the China-led Asian Infrastructure Investment Bank was established.

If the objective of profit maximisation is replaced with compassion or care for our brothers and sisters in humanity, the alternative to the IMF is to create an international development aid agency financed by channelling some 10% of the military budget of major military powers to that agency for the purpose of providing development aid, rather than conditional loans. This arrangement can also be executed by the individual development agencies of rich countries. This kind of arrangement will not be welcomed by the military-industrial complex and the deep state. Since these institutions of war always win, it is unlikely that something like this will materialise any time soon.

An interesting suggestion on what to do with the IMF is given by MacFarland (2006), who proposes to retain the IMF but move it into the

Pentagon (or the CIA or the Treasury). The rationale for this recommendation is that "the IMF is an important weapon in our national defense". He is absolutely right in characterising the situation as follows: "if we are unhappy with a foreign country, we can send in the military" but "if we are really unhappy, we can send in the IMF". After all, who could have imagined that the IMF would be used to force Julian Assange out of the Ecuadorian embassy in London?

REFERENCES

Abouharb, R., & Cingranelli, D. (2007). *Human Rights and Structural Adjustment*. Cambridge: Cambridge University Press.

Adusei, A. (2009, May 30). IMF and World Bank: Agents of Poverty or Partners of Development?. https://www.modernghana.com/news/219270/imf and world-bank-agents-of-poverty-or-partners-of-develop.html

Aiyar, S. S. A. (1994, July 24). Critics Want IMF, World Bank Abolished. http://swaminomics.org/critics-want-imf-world-bank-abolished/

Akyüz, Y. (2005, September 16). Reforming the IMF: Back to the Drawing Board, Paper Presented at a G-24 Meeting in the IMF. http://www.mfa.gov.tr/reforming-the-imf_-back-to-the-drawing-board-.tr.mfa

Anderson, S. (2005). IMF: Reform, Downsize, or Abolish. http://fpif.org/imf_reform_downsize_or_abolish/

Babb, S. (2005). The Social Consequences of Structural Adjustment: Recent Evidence and Current Debates. *Annual Review of Sociology, 31*, 199–222.

Babb, S., & Carruthers, B. (2008). Conditionality: Forms, Function, and History. *Annual Review of Law and Social Science, 4*, 13–29.

Babb, S., & Kentikelenis, A. (2017). International Financial Institutions as Agents of Neoliberalism. In D. Cahill, M. Cooper, & M. Konings (Eds.), *The SAGE Handbook of Neoliberalism*. Thousand Oaks: SAGE.

Bandow, D. (1994). The IMF: A Record of Addiction and Failure. In D. Bandow & I. Vasquez (Eds.), *Perpetuating Poverty: The World Bank, the IMF, and the Developing World*. Washington, DC: Cato Institute.

Barro, R. J. (2000, April 10). If We Can't Abolish the IMF, Let's at Least Make Big Changes. *Business Week*.

Ben-Ami, D. (2011, May 30). Five Reasons the IMF Should Be Abolished. http://www.realclearmarkets.com/2011/05/30/five_reasons_the_imf_should_be_abolished_114239.html

Bhide, A., & Phelps, E. (2011, July 11). More Harm Than Good: How the IMF's Business Model Sabotages Properly Functioning Capitalism. *Newsweek*.

Bird, G. (1995). *IMF Lending to Developing Countries: Issues and Evidence*. London: Routledge.

Bird, G. (2001). A Suitable Case for Treatment? Understanding the Ongoing Debate about the IMF. *Third World Quarterly, 22*, 823–848.

Bird, G. (2003). *The IMF and the Future: Issues and Options Facing the Fund.* London: Routledge.

Desai, M. (2014, October 6). Reform the IMF, or Just Abolish it. https://www.financialexpress.com/archive/reform-the-imf-or-just-abolish-it/1295757/

Donnan, S., & Dyer, G. (2015, March 17). US Warns of Loss of Influence over China Bank. *Financial Times.*

Dreher, A. (2006). IMF and Economic Growth: The Effects of Programs, Loans, and Compliance with Conditionality. *World Development, 34*, 769–788.

Dugger, C. (2007, December 2). Ending Famine Simply by Ignoring the Experts. *New York Times.*

Edwards, S. (1989). The International Monetary Fund and the Developing Countries: A Critical Evaluation. NBER Working Papers, No. 2909.

Eichengreen, B. (2009). Out-of-the-Box Thoughts on the International Financial System. IMF Working Papers, No. 09-116.

Frenkel, M., & Menkhoff, L. (2000, May/June). An Analysis of Competing IMF Reform Proposals. *Intereconomics*, 107–113.

Friedman, M. (1998, October 13). Markets to the Rescue. *Wall Street Journal.*

Gauding, M. (2011, July 19). Solution to World Poverty: Abolish the World Bank and the IMF. http://occasionalplanet.org/2011/07/19/solution-to-world-poverty-abolish-the-world-bank-and-the-imf/

Hanke, S. H. (1998). How to Establish Monetary Stability in Asia. *Cato Journal, 17*, 295–301.

Hanke, S. H. (2000, April 13). Abolish the IMF. *Forbes.*

Huber, E., Mustillo, T., & Stephens, J. D. (2008). Politics and Social Spending in Latin. *American Journal of Politics, 70*, 420–436.

IMF. (2000). Reforming the IMF: Progress Since Prague 2000. https://www.imf.org/external/np/exr/ib/2002/120502.htm

International Economy. (2007, Spring). A Symposium of Views: Is the IMF Obsolete?, 12–23.

Johnson, B. T., & Schaefer, B. D. (1997, May 6). The International Monetary Fund: Outdated, Ineffective, and Unnecessary. Heritage Foundation Backgrounder No. 1113.

Kain, E. (2011, May 20). Should We Abolish the IMF? *Forbes.*

Kentikelenis, A. E., Stubbs, T. H., & King, L. P. (2016). IMF Conditionality and Development Policy Space, 1985–2014. *Review of International Political Economy, 23*, 543–582.

Khan, M. S. (1990). The Macroeconomic Effects of Fund-Supported Adjustment Programs. *IMF Staff Papers, 37*, 195–231.

Krishnan, G. (2016, May 15). Exposing The IMF and World Bank – Organizations that are Systematically Controlling and Crippling the World Economy Through

Neoliberalism.   https://www.linkedin.com/pulse/exposing-imf-world-bank-organizations-controlling-economy-krishnan

Kumar, M. (2018, July 21). Ecuador to Withdraw Asylum for WikiLeaks Founder Julian Assange. https://thehackernews.com/2018/07/wikileaks-julian-assange-ecuador-asylum.html

MacFarland, J. H. (2006, September 26). Comment. https://marginalrevolution.com/marginalrevolution/2006/09/should_we_aboli.html

Metinsoy, S., & Angin, M. (2017, November 17–18). IMF Programmes and Democracy. The 2017 IPES Conference, University of Texas at Austin.

Moosa, I. A. (2012). *The US-China Trade Dispute: Facts, Figures and Myths.* Cheltenham: Edward Elgar.

Moosa, N. (2018). The Consequences of IMF Conditionality for Government Expenditure on Health. *Management and Economics Research Journal, 4,* 38–47.

Mwakikagile, G. (2006). *Africa is in a Mess: What Went Wrong and What Should be Done.* Dar es Salaam: New Africa Press.

Nelson, S. C., & Wallace, G. P. R. (2017). Are IMF Lending Programs Good or Bad for Democracy? *Review of International Organizations, 12,* 523–558.

Oatley, T., & Yackee, J. (2004). American Interests and IMF Lending. *International Politics, 41,* 415–429.

Oberdabernig, D. (2013). Revisiting the Effects of IMF Programs on Poverty and Inequality. *World Development, 46,* 113–142.

Oxfam. (2000, April). Reforming the IMF. Oxfam Policy Papers. https://www.globalpolicy.org/component/content/article/209/43155.html

Oxfam. (2002). Death on the Doorstep of the Summit. Oxfam Briefing Papers, No. 29.

Reinhart, C. M., & Trebesch, C. (2016). The International Monetary Fund: 70 Years of Reinvention. *Journal of Economic Perspectives, 30,* 3–28.

Sachs, J. D. (1989). Strengthening IMF Programs in Highly Indebted Countries. In C. Gwin & R. E. Feinberg (Eds.), *The International Monetary Fund in a Multipolar World: Pulling Together.* New Brunswick: Transaction Books.

Stiglitz, J. (2002). *Globalization and its Discontents.* New York: Norton.

Stubbs, T., Kentikelenis, A., Stuckler, D., McKee, M., & King, L. (2017). The Impact of IMF Conditionality on Government Health Expenditure: A Cross-National Analysis of 16 West African Nations. *Social Science and Medicine, 174,* 220–227.

Torres, H. (2007). Reforming the International Monetary Fund—Why its Legitimacy is at Stake. *Journal of International Economic Law, 10,* 443–460.

Truman, E. (2008). On What Terms is the IMF Worth Funding? Peterson Institute for International Economics, Working Papers, No. WP 08-11.

van Reybrouck, D. (2012). *Congo: The Epic History of a People.* New York: Harper-Collins.

Yeager, L. B. (1998). How to Avoid International Financial Crises. *Cato Journal, 17,* 257–265.

CHAPTER 7

Epilogue

7.1 A Portrayal of a Fund Mission

A delegation of IMF staff residing in Washington, DC and earning tax-free, inflation-proof salaries arrives in the capital of a poor country requiring financial assistance. Upon their arrival they are taken to the only five-star hotel in town to relax following a long flight—first class, of course. The mission starts by lecturing the officials of the poor country on the benefits of privatisation, liberalisation and deregulation, which they must indulge in to be part of the "free world". They are preached on the blessings that will be bestowed on the people of that country by the almighty market, the very reason for peace and prosperity in "western" countries. The helpless officials are then handed documents to sign, declaring allegiance to the almighty market and promising to follow the IMF advice without the slightest deviation. They are also warned to do so or else. While the IMF delegation is on its way back to DC, the citizens of the country they have just left are told that the price of bread will quadruple while their wages and pensions will be cut in half. A riot ensues, leading to death, injury and destruction of property. Things calm down after the intervention of the police, army, national guard and special forces. The saga starts all over again some two years later when the IMF delegation visits to check allegiance to the almighty market and recommends the privatisation of all hospitals.

Bad things happen and persist because of the presence of powerful beneficiaries. Wars persist because war is a profitable enterprise for the war

© The Author(s) 2019
I. A. Moosa, N. Moosa, *Eliminating the IMF*,
https://doi.org/10.1007/978-3-030-05761-9_7

profiteers of the military-industrial complex. Almost a hundred years ago, General Smedley Butler described war as a "racket" and raised the slogan "to hell with war". He described immaculately the winners, the military suppliers who made huge profits out of America's participation in World War I and the losers who paid with life and limb or (if lucky) survived life in rat-infested trenches under non-stop bombardment. Likewise, IMF riots persist because the misery of the protestors is paralleled by the huge profits made by multinationals as they acquire public assets, fertile land and natural resources for almost nothing.

The IMF was established to perform a function that has been unnecessary since 1971, the supervision of the Bretton Woods system of fixed exchange rates. But if the Fund were abolished, what would happen to the poor countries needing development assistance? How about diverting funds from the military-industrial complex to development aid? This can be done by allocating 10% of the military budgets of rich countries to unconditional development aid. We owe this to our brothers and sisters in humanity, and owe nothing to the military-industrial complex.

7.2   Regime Change

In his interview with Palast (2001), Joseph Stiglitz argued that the IMF/World Bank programmes produce a huge number of losers (the very people the programmes are supposed to help) but the clear winners, according to Stiglitz, "seem to be the western banks and US Treasury". Stiglitz has two concerns about these programmes: (i) they undermine democracy because they are designed in secrecy and driven by an absolutist (neoliberal) ideology, and hence they are never open for discourse or dissent; and (ii) they do not work. In fact, it is not only that they do not work—they may lead to catastrophic consequences. For example, Stiglitz refers to the "guiding hand of IMF structural assistance" that produced a 23% drop in Africa's income. Yet, Botswana avoided this fate by telling the IMF to "go packing". Unfortunately, the "go packing" solution does not always work, as resistance to IMF-like policies can be met with lethal force.

In 1956, President Nassir of Egypt nationalised the Suez Canal for the benefit of his own people as the Canal provided (and still provides) substantial revenue for the country. Nationalisation is the opposite of privatisation, and hence it cannot be good for the people according to the Washington Consensus. To defend the people of Egypt from Nassir, who "killed his own people", Britain and France (the "western democracies") decided to kill more of his people by attacking the country in a grotesque act of aggression. In 1953, the democratically elected government of Iran nationalised the oil sector, soon to be toppled by foreign intervention, followed by the installation of a despot who was friendlier to foreign oil companies—in that case, it did not matter that the despot killed his own people. In 1973, a coup was orchestrated in Chile by the CIA to protect the interests of American Telephone and Telegraph (AT&T). That coup (the Chilean 9/11) resulted in the killing of hundreds of thousands of people. More recently, regime changes (successful and unsuccessful) were orchestrated in Iraq, Libya, Ukraine, Venezuela and Syria because those in power did not agree with the Washington preachers. Regime change is initiated for the purpose of policy changes in the direction of the Washington Consensus. Sometimes regime changes are executed or attempted by assassinating the incumbent head of state or government who does not subscribe to the Washington Consensus (a deceased example is Fidel Castro and a living example is Nicolás Maduro).

In any case, there is no difference between policy changes forced by bombing a country back to the Stone Age and those forced by the financial power of the IMF. Sometimes the two work together, where conditionality is enforced by military aggression. It was the US Air Force and Navy that bombed Iraq in 2003—yet it was the IMF that subsequently went in and recommended the immediate privatisation of everything under the sun, including (of course) the oil sector. Another recommendation was the removal of subsidies at a time when the people of what used to be a rich and prosperous secular country were living on government handouts after years of sanctions and brutal bombing of the infrastructure. At one time, Dick Cheney advocated the bombing of the electricity grid to give them (the people of Iraq) a harsh winter. This is the same Dick Cheney who benefited enormously from the operations of Kellogg Brown & Root (KBR), a subsidiary of Halliburton, in occupied Iraq.

7.3 Textbook Economics Versus Reality

The IMF attracts the best talent from around the world—after all, who does not want to earn a tax-free, inflation-proof salary while living in Washington, DC? More than two thousand economists work at the IMF, all of whom are trained in neoclassical economics and think on the same wavelength as they get indoctrinated so that they become good at defending IMF-prescribed policies. It is invariably the case that the IMF staff present textbook reasoning to the officials of an oppressed country without taking into account the particular conditions of the country—that is, they ignore reality to accomplish undeclared objectives.

One such example is the recommendation on the exchange rate regime made by the IMF team that visited Baghdad in June 2003. The first author of this book, who was then an advisor to the US Treasury, recommended the establishment of a currency board, which is the most appropriate regime for a country ravaged by war and hyperinflation. The IMF team did not like the idea and advocated managed floating as a more appropriate exchange rate arrangement. The IMF put forward a standard textbook case against the establishment of a currency board (and other fixed exchange rate arrangements) hinging on the following pillars: (i) the difficulty of managing external shocks, (ii) the requirement of a strong fiscal policy, and (iii) the possibility of serious consequences if an inappropriate level of the fixed exchange rate is selected. This is what students are told in an intermediate macroeconomics class.

While these arguments are fine in a general sense, it is inappropriate (to say the least) to put forward a proposition that does not take into account the specifics of the situation in Iraq and its priorities. To start with, the shocks argument is mostly applicable to a developed country with a diversified export base, not to a country that derives 95% of its foreign exchange revenue from a commodity that is priced in US dollar terms. Second, a strong fiscal policy would be an outcome of a currency board, because this arrangement prevents the monetisation of the budget deficit. Third, serious consequences would arise if the wrong level of the exchange rate is chosen, which is the rule rather than the exception.

Consider the following arguments against managed floating for the particular case of occupied Iraq. First, managed floating requires intervention in the foreign exchange market, which the staff of the Central Bank of Iraq could not handle. Second, a priority for Iraq was a stable currency, both internally and externally, an objective that is best achieved by the establishment of a currency board, not through managed floating. Third, a currency board is more conducive to the restoration of the credibility of the Central Bank of Iraq. Fourth, managed floating with little reserves encourages speculative attacks on the currency.

On the other hand, the establishment of a currency board can be advocated on the following grounds. First, a currency board for Iraq should not be looked at as something that precludes a macroeconomic policy tool, the exchange rate, but rather as an arrangement that produces a stable currency, restores the credibility of the central bank and precludes the tendency to indulge in deficit financing. Second, it was a matter of priorities, and the setting of priorities for Iraq required the discipline provided by a currency board. Third, a currency board is an extreme measure, but it was needed to deal with an extreme situation resulting from years of macroeconomic mis-management, let alone war and sanctions. In any case there was no harm in considering a shift from the currency board to something else in the future, once conditions have changed.

In terms of costs and benefits, one would tend to think that under the conditions prevailing then, there was no viable alternative for a currency board as the exchange rate arrangement for Iraq. Yet the IMF won and Iraq adopted managed floating despite the lack of economic sense in this policy recommendation.

7.4   DISMAL FAILURE OR SPECTACULAR SUCCESS?

Most people think that the invasion and occupation of Iraq was a dismal failure from an Anglo-American perspective because the declared objectives were not met. The objective of eliminating weapons of mass destruction was not met because there were no weapons of mass destruction. The objective of turning Iraq into a vibrant democracy was not met because Iraq is now a failed state with rampant corruption, sectarian strife and crime the likes of which have never been seen before (such as kidnapping for ransom). The objective of making the world safer was not met because the world was safer before 2003. However, if the invasion of Iraq is judged by the undeclared objective of destabilising the country and the region as a whole, then it has been a spectacular success. If it is judged by the unde-clared objective of having enemies and engaging in perpetual war for the benefit of the deep state on behalf of the military-industrial complex, then it has been a spectacular success. And if it is judged by the objective of looting the country, then it has been a spectacular success.

The same can be said about the IMF. If the work of the IMF is judged by the declared objective of eradicating poverty, then it has been a dismal failure. If it is judged by the declared objective of boosting growth, then it has been a dismal failure. If it is judged by the declared objective of divert-ing more resources to social expenditure, then it has been a dismal failure. And if it is judged by the declared objective of raising the standard of living, then it has been a dismal failure. However, if it is judged by the undeclared objective of looting domestic assets, then it has been a spectacular success.

If it is judged by the undeclared objective of impoverishing developing countries to deny them independence, then it has been a spectacular success. If it is judged by the undeclared objective of imposing neoliberal, right- wing ideas on developing countries, then it has been a spectacular success. And if it is judged by the undeclared objective of giving the corporate west free access to sources of raw materials and markets, then it has been a spectacular success.

It seems that, unlike what most people think, the invasion of Iraq and IMF operations have set the standard for how to do things effectively, efficiently and successfully. It also seems that Joseph Stiglitz was wrong when he said that IMF programmes did not work. They work exactly as intended.

7.5   Stiglitz, Fischer, Summers and Lutzenberger

In the closing section we consider very briefly the views of four major participants in the IMF-World Bank debate, ending up on a sombre note. In his review of Stiglitz's masterpiece, *Globalization and Its Discontents*, Friedman (2002) lists elegantly the arguments put forward by Stiglitz against the IMF, suggesting that "Stiglitz's indictment of the IMF and its policies is more than just an itemized bill of particulars" and that, as he puts it, "there is a coherence to this set of individual policies, that the failings of which he accuses the IMF are not just random mistakes". He then tries to present a rebuttal of Stiglitz's arguments but he does not do a good job.

Friedman implies that the arguments put forward by Stiglitz are polemic by arguing that "Stiglitz has presented, as effectively as it is possible to imagine anyone making it, his side of the argument". While he regards Stiglitz's book as a "challenge", Friedman thinks that someone must take up the challenge by writing the best possible book laying out the other sides of the argument. Whoever takes up the challenge, according to Friedman, must be "someone who thinks and writes as clearly as Stiglitz does, and who understands the underlying economic theory as well as he does, and who has a firsthand command of the facts of recent experience comparable to his". Friedman suggests two names for this mission (impossible). The first is Stanley Fischer, who was at one time the IMF's second in command and who "actually set the direction of the organization's policies". This is the same Stan Fischer who in June 2003 recommended a shock therapy for occupied Iraq, the immediate removal of all subsidies and a wholesale privatisation programme. Such a recommendation could not have been motivated by sound economics or the desire to improve the livelihood of millions of Iraqis who had endured years of oppression, sanctions and two rounds of brutal bombing, with oppression intensifying under a ruthless military occupation.

The second name suggested by Friedman was Larry Summers, who is an advocate of keeping the Fund as is because, by his own admission, the Fund has been serving US interests very well. This is the same Larry Summers who looks at the developing world with contempt. In a comment on pollution and prostate cancer in Africa, Summers said the following in a 1991 internal memo when he was the chief economist of the World Bank (Ismi 2004):

> Just between you and me, shouldn't the World Bank be encouraging more migration of the dirty industries to the LDCs [less-developed countries]? … I think the economic logic behind dumping a load of toxic waste in the lowest wage country is impeccable and we should face up to that … I've always thought that underpopulated countries in Africa are vastly under-polluted, their air quality is probably vastly inefficiently low compared to Los Angeles or Mexico City. … The concern over an agent that causes a one in a million change in the odds of prostate cancer is obviously going to be much higher in a country where people survive to get prostate cancer than in a country where under 5 mortality is 200 per thousand.

When the memo became public in February 1992, José Lutzenberger, Brazil's Secretary of the Environment at the time, wrote to Summers to say the following:

> Your reasoning is perfectly logical but totally insane. … Your thoughts [provide] a concrete example of the unbelievable alienation, reductionist thinking, social ruthlessness and the arrogant ignorance of many conventional economists' concerning the nature of the world we live in. … If the World Bank keeps you as vice president it will lose all credibility. To me it would confirm what I often said … the best thing that could happen would be for the Bank to disappear.

One would expect, as the Brazilian minister did, that Larry Summers would be fired from the World Bank (at least for being politically incorrect), but that was not to be. Summers went on to become the US Treasury Secretary in the Clinton Administration and subsequently the president of

Harvard University. Stan Fischer went on to be vice chairman of the Federal Reserve and the governor of the Bank of Israel. José Lutzenberger was fired, soon after writing the letter to Summers, for daring to question his attitude towards Africa and the developing world in general. Joseph Stiglitz, who was the World Bank's chief economist during the period 1997–2000, was also fired for daring to criticise the sister organisations.

This string of events can only happen in a mad, mad world, an expression that is borrowed from the title of an otherwise mediocre 1966 movie. Unfortunately, Krishnan (2016) is right in predicting that it is difficult to see a world without the IMF and World Bank because "they have established themselves over the years and today sit firmly at the top of the financial food chain in today's western world". This is the sombre note alluded to earlier.

REFERENCES

Friedman, B. (2002, August 15). Globalization: Stiglitz's Case. *The New York Review of Books*. https://www.nybooks.com/articles/2002/08/15/global-ization-stiglitzs-case/

Ismi, A. (2004). *Impoverishing a Continent: The World Bank and the IMF in Africa*. Halifax: The Halifax Initiative Coalition.

Krishnan, G. (2016, May 15). Exposing the IMF and World Bank – Organizations that are Systematically Controlling and Crippling the World Economy Through Neoliberalism. https://www.linkedin.com/pulse/exposing-imf-world-bank-organizations-controlling-economy-krishnan

Palast, G. (2001, April 29). IMF's Four Steps to Damnation. *The Guardian*. https://www.theguardian.com/business/2001/apr/29/business.mbas

INDEX